THE ROAD TO

ANCAPISTAN

AND ITS COST

D.K.N. Nielson

ISBN-13: 978-1544890999
ISBN-10: 1544890990

1

FORWARD

Anarchy in the minds of the masses is simply a form of chaos. This is believed by most people because human beings appreciate organization, which is what the brain does for us to varying degrees. Concepts, ideas, thoughts, they are all organized and processed; we hold on to things that we find beneficial and discard what is of no use. Determining all of this is very Anarchist of us and yet not all that chaotic most of the time. To suggest that some people cannot organize and process thought doesn't mean that most people are chaotic... it means that some are.

Anarchy is not a state of chaos; it is a state of having no rulers and no masters. Specifically it is the state of YOU being the master and ruler of yourself, much like you are with your mind. The Anarchist does not believe that you cease being in control of yourself outside of your mind, we believe that we still have that authority and the consequences associated.

INTRODUCTION

The chaos concept in Anarchy has been brought on mostly by the masquerade of communism. If anarchy is brought about under the idea that those who have, should be sharing; it is probably not anarchy at all... but communism. The pure communist uses the state to take from those who have and give to others, whereas the ANCOM (Anarcho Communist) will physically take from you, use or distribute the wealth and call what they are doing Anarchy when it is really communism... even chaos.

Anarchy is simply the philosophy that we do not require rulers... it literally means, Without Rulers. This book is about the specific concepts of Anarchy associated with the Black and Yellow, Taxation Is Theft, Anarcho Capitalist (ANCAP); anarchists. It is not meant to sway your thinking toward that school of thought, although I hope that it can do so from time to time. It is actually meant to provide clear steps and motions to take us in that direction while offering evidences why we should be going there.

To clarify, an ANCAP is someone who has determined that they do not require a leader, master, or ruler, and they believe that this freedom is represented fully in commerce. That business should be free to operate how they see fit and that people have the right to free exchange voluntarily among one another. The staple for the ANCAP is the idea that free enterprises solve all of the problems society faces by innovating new ways to approach civilization.

The best part is, Ancapistan actually creates an environment where virtually all forms of government are permissible within her boarders; so long as the members of the community enter voluntarily into the contract. This is something that no other form of government allows, they most certainly will not allow for a free society, who voluntarily chooses not to pay tribute in the form of taxes, it is always forced upon the citizens.

CONTENTS

Ownership

There Is One Law

Take a NAP

Criminals

Territorial Imperative

Financial Statements

OWNERSHIP

SELF OWNERSHIP

It begins with understanding ownership. This is a concept lost on the minds of a people who are in fact extremely selfish. The contradiction here is in the personality of the generation we are starting with. They are both encouraged to desire worthless things while possessing no ability to account for or control their own being. In other words, it belongs to me... but I am responsible for nothing... the blame belongs to another.

I submit that IT does not actually belong to you... not yet anyway. It can belong to you but first you have to recognize who you belong to. In the case of the citizen of country A which demands tribute in the form of a tax (of any kind) you belong to them. It doesn't matter how much freedom they tell you that you have, you still belong to them. Some farmers shove their animals in small cages with deplorable living conditions. Other farmers allow their animals huge pastures, even free range.

The animal still belongs to the farmer and its life and liberty are subjected to the whims of the farmer at any given time. When usefulness and necessity outrun productivity and purpose the animal is disposed of in some fashion or another. That is the economics of farming and this callousness is one reason why so many vegans have popped up in recent years. There is nothing inherently wrong with this callousness it is simply the way property is handled. Well you and I are like human cattle in many ways. The state has authority over us in the same way a cattle rustler claims authority over animals. In some cases the cattle rustler may actually go out and steal animals much like land owners did before the abolishment of human slavery. Other times the rustler will simply claim a free range animal who wanders onto its property. In both cases the creature becomes the property of the captors.

    Most citizens of country A do not actually feel like they are owned by anyone and that is the genius of the design. If you have ever been to a zoo you know that the goal is to make the animal comfortable in its habitat. If the environment is too restrictive the animal will not act natural. Governments are designed to make the people comfortable in their natural habitat so that they act natural even if the environment is far from natural. In this case the natural state of man is to be in control of his own self. The state will tell you that you *are* in control of yourself but it will also use force and coercion to keep you within the confines of their environmental boundaries. Sometimes these boundaries are not even physical; they reach inside of your being and absorb you on a mental and spiritual level turning you into the type of person you are supposed to be, while defining for you the type of person you are to avoid; both in yourself and around you. This sort of deep brainwashing can be overcome but it takes serious debugging.

Each of us can begin the process of obtaining freedom in the same place and thus urge others to also begin here. You were not born as an act of your will but the will of your parents. This is precisely why they have authority over you while you are growing up. This right of parents to govern their household must not be infringed upon in any society who claims to be free. It is in fact the only time that a monopoly on force exists and it is in place for a very important yet two fold reason. The child is incapable of surviving without help. This reason is the most important one to recognize, it is not conjecture; human children actually require others for their survival and to varying degrees for their upbringing. I have heard many say that this monopoly on force removes my right to claim AnCap as my political position but in the case of a young child you must come to accept that they are in fact not the equal of the parent. It is the parent's duty to raise them to be equals or even better examples but it must begin with some basis of authority that the parent holds. If the parent does not wield this authority the child will consider themselves equal and soon become a controlling tyrant in the home as many children have these days.

9

The second reason for this monopoly on force in parenting is to allow the generations to come to at least some concept of a life that is restrictive. It is one thing for the third or fourth generation to hear about the reasons we should protect our sovereignty and an entirely different thing to actually have an observable time in which we received that sovereignty we are so vehemently defending. It is akin to a rite of passage that will allow the individual to truly measure their freedom against an experience. This is not to say that a tyrannical parent is valued in a free society, but that all restriction, no matter how slight carries the potential to be tyrannical. It is a fact that some homes will continue their tyranny beyond the borders of their living spaces and into communities of their creation but those adults who enjoy membership MUST be willingly engaged in the practice and in no way forced to comply. You can however turn your sovereignty over at your will and discretion.

As for the children they are subjected to the government of the parents and will eventually be free to form their own government of their choosing. It is the parent who should prescribe the age of culpability and it is understood that different parents will allow sovereignty at different ages but as a whole the society must have a minimum and maximum threshold that is voluntarily agreed upon. This is to ensure that infants and toddlers are not recognized as sovereign citizens while at the same time that 30 year olds are not forced to stay at home.

The standard in our society for sovereignty in our current times is right around 18 years of age. In some ways this is arbitrary but in others it makes sense. People mature at different ages and in different stages but around the age of 18 the human is fully mature. There will no doubt be some mental maturity left to occur and maybe even a growth spurt here and there but we are erring on the side of caution by giving them sovereignty during this age. Perhaps the minimum could be 17 and the maximum would be 20. This gives the parent a window of three years to grant full sovereignty to the budding citizen.

At the point of sovereignty the child becomes the owner of themselves. This is the key to all ownership. You cannot possess anything if you do not actually have full and total possession of you. This is where all adult citizens in country A belong; they must come to the conclusion that they own themselves. If you come to the conclusion that you and you alone have the express right to govern yourself than you are ready to learn the parameters of that ownership of which much of this book will be dedicated.

Before we traverse that territory lets prove that we are in fact sovereign creatures by design. In order to do this we must come to terms with dependency. Humans are dependent upon four things respectively; oxygen, water, food, and shelter. In this age Oxygen is the most available of the four, to a lesser degree water is easily available, next food, and finally shelter. All of these things are available to human beings on this planet, sometimes it helps when we work together to obtain and have these things, other times it is our connections that actually limit our ability to enjoy them. Whatever the case may be in your current social paradigm, a human being has all of the necessary built in resources it takes to provide these things for themselves if they were alone on this planet. In other words we are not REALLY dependent on any sort of social system for survival. The same cannot be said for the Bee or the Ant, and a number of other creatures in our eco system. They are dependent on one another for their survival throughout their life.

Having said that, we cannot perpetuate our species and growth without the existence of a male and female of our species, we would merely die off after our single existence. Yet this does not disprove self ownership as much as it fills that truth with value and responsibility. We are not required to perpetuate the species but if we choose not to the species cannot and will not exist. Individuals have self ownership as a natural state in their character since a level of independence exists within the species, yet we are rewarded with interdependence and a will to choose a mate or our own selfish desires. This inherent selfish desire is exactly what separates us as creatures that can and do own themselves. An animal uses instinct as its mode of perpetuation and survival; it is in some ways a slave to this driving force sometimes to its own undoing. Instinct will cause the male lion to risk his life in a battle for a mate; it is a force that will drive him to his death if he loses. A human will simply wander off and find another mate most of the time, they might not even have that strong of a drive to mate. People routinely press instinct away for the sake of other benefits that a lion would not even have the capacity to consider. All of this proves that humans actually are meant to own themselves, why else are they given an independent will?

VOLUNTARY EXCHANGE

Having come to the conclusion that we own ourselves we can now come to terms with how that affects our life. You cannot own anything until you own yourself, if you do not own yourself anything and everything you claim ownership over is subject to those who do own you. On the other hand everything that you own is under your control. You owning yourself means that you have control of whatever you produce. This does not mean that if you work for a restaurant you own the food that you cook. It actually means that you have contracted yourself with the restaurant owner to produce for them. You are trading your production for your pay... not the product itself.

If you are a citizen of country A you know that although you have contracted with the restaurant owner to exchange your efforts of production for income, country A will take a portion of this income for their usage. This is because they do not accept the fact that you own yourself. The government actually believes that they own you and because of that, they have the RIGHT to take a portion of your income that you have agreed to trade your time for, in order to support themselves and the things they think those efforts should be spent on. If they own you, than the money is theirs to begin with and they are allowing you to have a portion. That makes you a slave to these owners. If you own yourself, than they are stealing from you. It is an important distinction.

Owning yourself means that you are able to freely contract with anyone over virtually anything. It does not mean that you are not responsible for the results of these contracts; you are in fact more responsible because there are fewer loopholes to free you from a blunder. Of course the extent and reach of a contract is based upon continued mutual agreement, there is no force that should be enacted to hold someone to a contract after its benefit is nullified by any party which adversely means that it is important that the contract is one that can be enforced by both parties before the terms are entered.

Self ownership also allows for property ownership. Property is anything that you obtain through free and voluntary exchange without violating the freedom or self ownership of another or his freely obtained property. You are completely free as an individual who owns himself and his property to both buy and sell property from others without any restriction upon you or them so far as you are both entering into the exchange voluntarily. You are not obligated to accept any form of pay that you do not want to accept and you cannot force anyone to accept any currency you choose. The entire transaction must begin and end as a voluntary agreement between all parties involved. The transaction and all agreements are binding so far as the individuals involved agree upon the conditions at the time of the transaction and no one has the right to change the circumstances after the exchange so far as no stipulation was previously made and agreed upon.

Voluntary exchange is the basis for the capitalist side of anarchy. Without free exchange you cannot call yourself anarchist because you are obviously restricted by whatever governing authority is enforcing the edict that free exchange is unlawful. This does not mean that a citizen of Ancapistan cannot submit themselves to authority; it is only that they are limiting their ownership and politically adjusting their position under the terms of that voluntary contract.

We live in a world full of people who actually cannot fathom the idea of voluntary and free exchange. There are literally thousands of strawman arguments designed to illicit the dangers of people living in a world that allows for such authority. I have had at least one person argue that I merely want a world where the local hot dog shop sells fingers in a bun. The absolute disconnection with thought that it takes to come up with such an argument astounds me but then again I must recognize that the state is very effective in promoting their necessity to the public.

To address that argument I would ask two questions, does anyone want to eat fingers? Who are supplying the fingers? Without regulation on a grand scale we suspect that nefarious people will be constantly trying to harm us. What this thinking fails to recognize is that nefarious people who want to harm us already exist and they either find a way around the regulation or simply hide the behavior from the regulators. So if you suspect that the soup you just ate was filled with something disgusting stop eating it. There is no assurance that it wasn't tainted simply because they are stamped with a government seal. That thinking also neglects the idea that state compliance can be as nefarious as the chef, and even worse than the chef if there is ANY possibility that his testing practices can be bought with a bribe. These concerns exist within any society and the government does not stop them they merely decide which practices and who are acceptable.

Under a voluntary contract people could make a pretty good business built on a sound reputation of quality in the industry of quality assurance. The better a company is at having a reputation of promoting companies that use safe business practices the more sought out their approval will become for businesses who want customers. None of this is without problems and we can create arguments going back and forth all day that contain scenarios of all sorts... many people spend hours doing just that on social media, it isn't tough to find.

The point really comes down to where you draw the line in the sand in your life and how that line is drawn for other people. If you believe that you should be allowed to live your life free from restrictions and that others should have the same freedom than you have to find a way to answer the problems society faces without FORCING people to comply. Every great business that exists is here because it has effectively solved a problem, individuals and those who come together and form companies solve problems all day every day. Individuals who come together to form governments create and talk about problems passing those on to the public rather than creatively solving them in a

way that benefits more than just a few.
They speak long about how every
program helps and we all benefit from
some program or another but it is
doublespeak designed to take you in so
many circles that you forget the truth;
they are stealing from your resources to
support someone else. They are doing
so because they believe that you are
too selfish to think of others and too
stupid to even find a solution if you
wanted to. Then after they degrade you
in this way they say, "You have a voice,
go and vote!" Great idea! Candidate A
wants to steal my money for schools,
Candidate B wants to steal my money for
military, candidate C wants to use a little
for both. Then you vote feeling
accomplished because you have chosen
the right form of theft and those morons
on the other sides will get less money.
Where is candidate V, the one who says,
"Taxation Is Theft, we don't need
government at all, lets become a society
who is responsible for ourselves and
just start selling everything off to private
companies. We can split all those profits
up equally among citizens and just start

over!" [The splitting of the profits sounds very communist until you recognize that the government was bought and paid for by citizens.

It is suggested to make a point and for a one time usage only, never to be applied to private property.]I'll tell you where he is, he was run out of Washington on a rail and even the people who he was trying to free simply laughed him off the podium. That is, if he ever existed at all. People need to WAKE UP before they can even handle their sovereignty because they don't really know what that would even look like. They don't necessarily understand that electing a candidate like this would result in his arrest for treason the first time he takes a step toward dismantling the government. Which by the way proves that even your vote is tainted, designed only to uphold the system as it currently exists rather than to remove it and start again.

In my early political reasoning's I was very constitutionalist believing that we merely needed to get back to those principles this country was founded upon in order to enjoy freedom again. Of course that age was not filled with freedom for all classes it was a quite specific class of gentlemen for the most part. This did not seem to dismay me as I merely resorted to our current definition of a citizen which seems in some ways to still be changing as people wonder what gender they actually are, take pains at defining life, and seem to be humanizing all sorts of creatures that scientifically have been previously understood as animal. What I failed to see was pointed out through closer observation of the Declaration of Independence.

We hold these truths to be self evident: [The following should be easily understood by everyone.] *that all men are created equal; that they are endowed by their creator with unalienable rights;* [All men were born with certain things that cannot be taken away or given away by anyone.] *that among these are life, liberty, and the pursuit of happiness:* [Here are a few of

23

those things; life, liberty, and the pursuit of happiness.]

It's this part of the document that really is not problematic. I highlight it to show you what most American's agree with and I put the bold definition following as my fair interpretation. Feel free to challenge that interpretation but read it by itself taking in the way that document reads in plain modern English. Let's read on:

-That to secure these rights, governments are instituted among men, **[In order to secure these things we need governments to protect them]** *deriving their just powers from the consent of the governed,* **[our powers are only justified by your consent.]**

If you are wondering about my point I am calling into question the actual need for a government to secure these things. Let's place some additional focus on two key words in the document that are generally overlooked by the average reader, **UNALIENABLE** and

SECURE. Unalienable means quite simply, **IMPOSSIBLE TO TAKE AWAY OR GIVE UP.** On the other hand secure in this sense; since it is being used as verb means, **TO MAKE SAFE.** How can you logically make safe something that cannot be taken away? In other words, if we have come so far as to agree that our rights **CANNOT BE TAKEN AWAY** Because they are that valuable and that important, why do we then need to add that we need to make them safe, who are we making them safe from if we already agree they are the most important things? (HINT: GOVERNMENTS!)

Well of course people lose their life, liberty, and the opportunity to pursue happiness all the time so we know that they are not safe, but it was the attempt of Thomas Jefferson to drive in the point that they needed to be understood as the true default of the human being born into this world. Man is **born free** and his whole being is actually constituted for that freedom. So let's organize ourselves to make sure that his freedoms are as secure as they can be. This is the reason for the government; its only real purpose in fact. Thomas

Jefferson knew this but the problem is that the government this philosophy created still had enough power to slowly take away the liberties it was designed to protect. This means that governments are powerless to protect liberty and only useful at limiting and removing it. Certainly there are varying degrees of this decrease in liberty as time and circumstance reduces sovereignty but it turns out the same. The document continues, recognizing this possibility and providing a solution.

--That whenever any Form of Government becomes destructive of these ends, **[If governments are not protecting individual freedoms]** *it is the Right of the People to alter or to abolish it, and to institute new Government,* **[Feel free then to altar or abolish the government]** *laying its foundation on such principles and organizing its powers in such form, as to them shall seem most likely to effect their Safety and Happiness.* **[Make sure whatever you replace it with does protect freedom, and self ownership.]**

Prudence, indeed, will dictate that Governments long established should not be changed for light and transient causes; [Be careful that you don't ruin a good thing over a minor problem;] *and accordingly all experience hath shewn, that mankind are more disposed to suffer, while evils are sufferable, than to right themselves by abolishing the forms to which they are accustomed.* [of course it is our experience that men will suffer a long time through all sorts of things before taking on a task as big as altering or abolishing a government that they are used to dealing with.] *But when a long train of abuses and usurpations, pursuing invariably the same Object evinces a design to reduce them under absolute Despotism,* [but come on, you can only take so much for so long when the entire goal is to put you under total control and tyranny.] *it is their right, it is their duty, to throw off such Government, and to provide new Guards for their future security.*[in a case like that it is the right and duty of men to get rid of the bastards and start fresh.] *--Such has been the patient sufferance of these*

27

Colonies; and such is now the necessity which constrains them to alter their former Systems of Government. [This is where we are NOW this is how we feel NOW; and NOW is the time for us to shed our old government.] *The history of the present King of Great Britain is a history of repeated injuries and usurpations, all having in direct object the establishment of an absolute Tyranny over these States. To prove this, let Facts be submitted to a candid world.* [The history of our current ruler and many predecessors is filled with repeated injustice and the desire to control every aspect of our lives, to in fact claim ownership over the citizens. These are not just words, they are provable facts that we will present.]

On the following points I will merely try to define a few things that could today compare with these complaints. Again, feel free to consider some on your own in order to understand the spirit of the original document.

He has refused his Assent to Laws, the most wholesome and necessary for the public good. [We cannot self govern, even when we ask permission we are denied.]

He has forbidden his Governors to pass Laws of immediate and pressing importance, unless suspended in their operation till his Assent should be obtained; and when so suspended, he has utterly neglected to attend to them. [No one can grant us the permission we need to govern ourselves.]

He has refused to pass other Laws for the accommodation of large districts of people, unless those people would relinquish the right of Representation in the Legislature, a right inestimable to them and formidable to tyrants only. [We cannot obtain permission through any means for the things we need to do, but we are always being forced to give up more of our rights and to pay more taxes.]

He has called together legislative bodies at places unusual, uncomfortable, and distant from the depository of their public Records, for the sole purpose of fatiguing them into compliance with his measures. [It is all but impossible to even find someone in a government position who can help you with anything, they always pass the buck.]

He has dissolved Representative Houses repeatedly, for opposing with manly firmness his invasions on the rights of the people. [Citizens are spied upon by government agencies, and people are thrown in prison or even killed for doing the things they want to do such as growing certain plants, not paying taxes, or using a currency that they prefer.]

He has refused for a long time, after such dissolutions, to cause others to be elected; whereby the Legislative powers, incapable of Annihilation, have returned to the People at large for their exercise; the State remaining in the mean time exposed to all the dangers of invasion from without, and convulsions within. [You can't change any of this from the inside because you have to be an insider to get in... and that doesn't make sense.]

He has endeavoured to prevent the population of these States; for that purpose obstructing the Laws for Naturalization of Foreigners; refusing to

30

pass others to encourage their migrations hither, and raising the conditions of new Appropriations of Lands. [We do not have clear property rights in place which come from our right to ourselves only and therefore our governance of our various properties that we as individuals freely own are constantly restricted. Not only that, we are not allowed to freely trade among one another without restrictions limiting those voluntary trade agreements.]

He has obstructed the Administration of Justice, by refusing his Assent to Laws for establishing Judiciary powers. [We cannot establish a justice system which applies only to victims, there are thousands of laws that have virtually victimless crimes being committed which result in fines, restrictions, and imprisonment toward people that have violated no ones rights.]

He has made Judges dependent on his Will alone, for the tenure of their offices, and the amount and payment of their salaries. [Members of congress and other politicians routinely give themselves raises that the tax payer is responsible for.]

He has erected a multitude of New Offices, and sent hither swarms of Officers to harrass our people, and eat out their substance. [Everywhere you go you see government officials, offices, industries, and police officers enforcing some new and arbitrary law that often has no victim. There are new powers granted to them and new police forces that are specialized in certain areas. They sit and wait for small infractions forcing people to pay in duties and fines.]

He has kept among us, in times of peace, Standing Armies without the Consent of our legislatures. [Many police forces are militarized and utilizing weapons only previously seen on battlefields. Many are so covert that you cannot tell they are police until they jump out weapons drawn.]

He has affected to render the Military independent of and superior to the Civil power. [The police can kill at will most of the time. They are given paid leave while they investigate themselves, routinely they are held to a different standard than a citizen would be, let off when they violate citizens rights.]

He has combined with others to subject us to a jurisdiction foreign to our constitution, and unacknowledged by our laws; giving his Assent to their Acts of pretended Legislation: [Our monetary system is criminal, money is printed by the federal reserve which is a private banking firm with a government sounding name and sold to the nation at interest having no value backing it whatsoever and yet we are compelled to accept it as valid.]

For Quartering large bodies of armed troops among us: [Our streets are filled with police and police agencies of which most we have no use.]

For protecting them, by a mock Trial, from punishment for any Murders which they should commit on the Inhabitants of these States: [Police can virtually do whatever they choose among us, killing citizens and manufacturing evidences, if they say you are guilty that is generally enough during a mock trial that convicts citizens and acquits government officials.]

For cutting off our Trade with all parts of the world: [We cannot own the things we want to own, products must be

approved by government agencies.
There are limits on medications, guns,
even natural resources.]

*For imposing Taxes on us without our
Consent:* [Production is taxed at every
single stage and the individual is often
taxed multiple times on his income.
Buying or selling nearly anything comes
with a tax, and the average person has
no idea what their tax money is funding.
You cannot even live on a piece of
property you own without paying a tax
for living there.]

*For depriving us in many cases, of the
benefits of Trial by Jury:* [The judicial
system is a joke, lawyers and judges all
know each other and treat the accused
like pawns in their game, profiting off of
misfortune. Prisons are designed to run
like a business so beds are filled mostly
with drug offenders in order to bring
industry to suffering towns, all paid for
with tax money.]

*For transporting us beyond Seas to be
tried for pretended offences* [Drug
offenders are not criminals but made
criminals because of stupid laws. No
action should result in loss of liberty that
has not first created a tangible victim.]

34

For abolishing the free System of English Laws in a neighbouring Province, establishing therein an Arbitrary government, and enlarging its Boundaries so as to render it at once an example and fit instrument for introducing the same absolute rule into these Colonies: [Foreign wars have been fought for decades disrupting the lives and well beings of people who would have nothing to do with the current government otherwise. Their actions have created enemies where there might not have been any, mostly for some special interest or personal profiteering on the tax payer's dime.]

For taking away our Charters, abolishing our most valuable Laws, and altering fundamentally the Forms of our Governments: [By denying self-ownership you make yourself an enemy to the individual.]

For suspending our own Legislatures, and declaring themselves invested with power to legislate for us in all cases whatsoever. [When taking away the individual's right to themselves you decide for them what they are allowed to do in many instances.]

35

He has abdicated Government here, by declaring us out of his Protection and waging War against us. [The responsibility of protecting us from threats to our resources from within your own ranks is an act of war against citizens.]

He has plundered our seas, ravaged our Coasts, burnt our towns, and destroyed the lives of our people. [The state has unilaterally determined what is theirs through use of force. Taxes are the most prominent form of theft, Eminent domain is the word used for taking what otherwise belongs to a citizen and using it how they see fit, even selling it. War is how they obtain it otherwise.]

He is at this time transporting large Armies of foreign Mercenaries to compleat the works of death, desolation and tyranny, already begun with circumstances of Cruelty & perfidy scarcely paralleled in the most barbarous ages, and totally unworthy the Head of a civilized nation. [Even now the state makes war on foreign nations without our consent and for their own purposes; even now they have soldiers ready to take a stand against citizens arming local law enforcements and training them to subdue any threats to the regime.]

He has constrained our fellow Citizens taken Captive on the high Seas to bear Arms against their Country, to become the executioners of their friends and Brethren, or to fall themselves by their Hands. [The state has asked for loyalty for their causes to the point of death, enlisting young men under ideals they would not surely die for but only kill for, or have others kill for. These men then act out against their own people on their own soil in order to collect revenue to support a system that most are weary of.]

He has excited domestic insurrections amongst us, and has endeavoured to bring on the inhabitants of our frontiers, the merciless Indian Savages, whose known rule of warfare, is an undistinguished destruction of all ages, sexes and conditions. [Riots have occurred on our own streets, and false flag attacks have brought threats of foreigners to our doorsteps, this kingdom is a war like kingdom and the leaders have violated our rights with aggression against us, of which we have a duty to respond.]

37

So let's read that plain English version straight through and see how it sounds to our modern ears.

The following should be easily understood by everyone: All men were born with certain things that cannot be taken away or given away by anyone. Here are a few of those things; life, liberty, and the pursuit of happiness. In order to secure these things we need governments to protect them but our powers are only justified by your consent. If we are not protecting individual freedoms, feel free to altar or abolish the government, Make sure that whatever you replace it with does protect freedom, and self ownership. Be careful that you don't ruin a good thing over a minor problem; of course it is our experience that men will suffer a long time through all sorts of things before taking on a task as big as altering or abolishing a government that they are used to dealing with, but come on, you can only take so much for so long when the entire goal is to put you under total control and tyranny. In a case like that it is the right and duty of men to get rid of the bastards and start fresh. This is where we are NOW this is how we feel NOW; and NOW is the time for us to shed our old government. The history of our current ruler and many predecessors is filled with repeated injustice and the desire to control every aspect of our lives, to in fact claim ownership over the citizens. These are not just words, they are provable facts that we will present.

We cannot self govern, even when we ask permission we are denied.

No one can grant us the permission we need to govern ourselves.

We cannot obtain permission through any means for the things we need to do, but we are always being forced to give up more of our rights and to pay more taxes.

It is all but impossible to even find someone in a government position who can help with anything, they always pass the buck.

Citizens are spied upon by government agencies, and people are thrown in prison or even killed for doing the things they want to do such as growing certain plants, not paying taxes, or using a currency that they prefer.

You can't change any of this from the inside because you have to be an insider to get in... and that doesn't make sense.

We do not have clear property rights in place which come from our right to ourselves only and therefore our governance of our various properties that we as individuals freely own are constantly restricted. Not only that, we are not allowed to freely trade among one another without restrictions limiting those voluntary trade agreements.

We cannot establish a justice system which applies only to victims, there are thousands of laws that have virtually victimless crimes being committed which result in fines, restrictions, and imprisonment toward people that have violated no one's rights.

Members of congress and other politicians routinely give themselves raises that the tax payer is responsible for.

Everywhere you go you see government officials, offices, industries, and police officers enforcing some new and arbitrary law that often has no victim. There are new powers granted to them and new police forces that are specialized in certain areas. They sit and wait for small infractions forcing people to pay in duties and fines.

Many police forces are militarized and utilizing weapons only previously seen on battlefields. Many are so covert that you cannot tell they are police until they jump out weapons drawn.

The police can kill at will most of the time. They are given paid leave while they investigate themselves, routinely they are held to a different standard than a citizen would be, let off when they violate citizens rights.

Our monetary system is criminal, money is printed by the federal reserve which is a private banking firm with a government sounding name and sold to the nation at interest having no value backing it whatsoever and yet we are compelled to accept it as valid.

Our streets are filled with police and police agencies of which most we have no use.

Police can virtually do whatever they choose among us, killing citizens and manufacturing evidences, if they say you are guilty that is generally enough during a mock trial that convicts citizens and acquits government officials.

We cannot own the things we want to own, products must be approved by government agencies. There are limits on medications, guns, even natural resources.

Production is taxed at every single stage and the individual is often taxed multiple times on his income. Buying or selling nearly anything comes with a tax, and the average person has no idea what their tax money is funding. You cannot even live on a piece of property you own without paying a tax for living there.

The judicial system is a joke, lawyers and judges all know each other and treat the accused like pawns in their game, profiting off of misfortune. Prisons are designed to run like a business so beds are filled mostly with drug offenders in order to bring industry to suffering towns, all paid for with tax money.

Drug offenders are not criminals but made criminals because of stupid laws. No action should result in loss of liberty that has not first created a tangible victim.

Foreign wars have been fought for decades disrupting the lives and well beings of people who would have nothing to do with the current government otherwise. Government's actions have created enemies where there might not have been any, mostly for some special interest or personal profiteering on the tax payer's dime.

By denying self-ownership the state makes themselves an enemy to the individual.

When taking away the individual's right to themselves you decide for them what they are allowed to do in many instances.

The responsibility of protecting us from threats to our resources from within government ranks is an act of war against citizens.

The state has unilaterally determined what is theirs through use of force. Taxes are the most prominent form of theft, Eminent domain is the word used for taking what otherwise belongs to a citizen and using it how they see fit, even selling it. War is how they obtain it otherwise.

Even now the government makes war on foreign nations without our consent and for their own purposes; even now they have soldiers ready to take a stand against citizens arming local law enforcements and training them to subdue any threats to the regime.

The state has asked for loyalty for their causes to the point of death, enlisting young men under ideals they would not surely die for but only kill for, or have others kill for. These men then act out against their own people on their own soil in order to collect revenue to support a system that most are weary of.

Riots have occurred on our own streets, and false flag attacks have brought threats of foreigners to our doorsteps, this kingdom is a war like kingdom and the leaders have violated our rights with aggression against us, of which we have a duty to respond.

It's not bad, when you see it that way, but I still believe it needs some revision. If it were going to be used today I would suggest we simply omit the part about governments being necessary. I also want to give my readers a few lines to add their thoughts on any of the points involved.

The following should be easily understood by everyone: All men were born with certain things that should not be taken away by force. Here are a few of those things; life, liberty, self ownership, and the pursuit of happiness. In order to secure these things we need people willing to protect themselves and others but only through voluntary consent. If they are not protecting individual freedoms, feel free to altar or abolish the contract, Make sure that whatever you replace it with does protect freedom and self ownership equally. Be careful that you don't ruin a good thing over a minor problem; of course it is our experience that men will suffer a long time through all sorts of things before taking on a task as big as altering or abolishing a government that they are used to dealing with, but come on, you can only take so much for so long when the entire goal is to put you under total control and tyranny. In a case like that it is the right and duty of men to get rid of the bastards and start fresh. This is where we are NOW this is how we feel NOW; and NOW is the time for us to shed our old government. The history of our current ruler and many predecessors is filled with repeated injustice and the desire to control every aspect of our lives, to in fact claim ownership over the citizens. These are not just words, they are provable facts that we will present.

_____
_____
_____
_____
_____
_____
_____
_____
_____

We are essentially slaves being denied
the right to self governance which
begins with self ownership.

_____
_____
_____
_____
_____
_____
_____
_____

We cannot obtain permission to self
govern from within this system because it
is designed to keep itself alive through
taxation which is theft.

_____
_____
_____
_____
_____
_____
_____
_____
_____
_____

Government officials are generally
unnecessary individuals who work only
for a pay check and cannot do their job
as effectively as the free market would
be forced to for its survival.

_____
_____
_____
_____
_____
_____
_____
_____
_____

Citizens are spied upon by government
agencies, and people are thrown in
prison or even killed for doing the
things they want to do such as growing

certain plants, not paying taxes, or using a currency that they prefer.

_____

_____

_____

_____

_____

_____

_____

_____

_____

You can't change any of this from the inside because you have to be an insider to get in... and that doesn't make sense.

_____

_____

_____

_____

_____

_____

_____

_____

_____

We do not have clear property rights in place which come from our right to ourselves only and therefore our governance of our various properties that we as individuals freely own are constantly restricted. Not only that, we are not allowed to freely trade among one another without restrictions limiting those voluntary trade agreements.

_____
_____
_____
_____
_____
_____
_____
_____
_____

We cannot establish a justice system which applies only to victims, there are thousands of laws that have virtually victimless crimes being committed which result in fines, restrictions, and imprisonment toward people that have violated no one's rights.

_____
_____
_____
_____
_____

_____
_____
_____
_____
_____

Members of congress and other politicians routinely give themselves raises that the tax payer is responsible for.

_____
_____
_____
_____
_____
_____
_____
_____
_____

Everywhere you go you see government officials, offices, industries, and police officers enforcing some new and arbitrary law that often has no victim. There are new powers granted to them and new police forces that are specialized in certain areas. They sit and wait for small infractions forcing people to pay in duties and fines.

_____
_____
_____
_____
_____
_____
_____
_____
_____
_____

Many police forces are militarized and utilizing weapons only previously seen on battlefields. Many are so covert that you cannot tell they are police until they jump out weapons drawn.

_____
_____
_____
_____
_____
_____
_____
_____
_____

The police can kill at will most of the time. They are given paid leave while they investigate themselves, routinely they are held to a different standard than a citizen would be, let off when they violate citizens rights.

———————————————
———————————————
———————————————
———————————————
———————————————
———————————————
———————————————
———————————————
———————————————
———————————————

Our monetary system is criminal, money is printed by the federal reserve which is a private banking firm with a government sounding name and sold to the nation at interest having no value backing it whatsoever and yet we are compelled to accept it as valid.

———————————————
———————————————
———————————————
———————————————
———————————————
———————————————
———————————————
———————————————
———————————————
———————————————

We have reason to believe that 911 was an inside job, that terror has been used against Americans for the purposes of which we can only guess.

Law enforcement can virtually do whatever they choose among us, killing citizens and manufacturing evidences, if they say you are guilty that is generally enough during a mock trial that convicts citizens and acquits government officials.

We cannot own the things we want to own, products must be approved by government agencies. There are limits on medications, guns, even natural resources. People have been jailed for collecting rain water, building on their own property, and defending themselves and their property from those who have no right to it.

_____

_____

_____

_____

_____

_____

_____

_____

_____

Production is taxed at every single stage and the individual is often taxed multiple times on his income. Buying or selling nearly anything comes with a tax, and the average person has no idea what their tax money is funding. You cannot even live on a piece of property you own without paying a tax for living there. You cannot even do what you want on this property without asking permission to do so.

The judicial system is a joke, lawyers and judges all know each other and treat the accused like pawns in their game, profiting off of misfortune. Prisons are designed to run like a business so beds are filled mostly with drug offenders in order to bring industry to suffering towns, all paid for with tax money.

Drug offenders are not criminals but made criminals because of stupid laws. No action should result in loss of liberty that has not first created a tangible victim.

Foreign wars have been fought for decades disrupting the lives and well beings of people who would have nothing to do with the current government otherwise. Government's actions have created enemies where there might not have been any, mostly for some special interest or personal profiteering on the tax payer's dime.

_____

_____

_____

_____

_____

_____

_____

_____

By denying self-ownership the state
makes themselves an enemy to the
individual. They call the citizen a criminal
who wants to do things that do not
create or result in victims but this man is
only a criminal because the state exists.

_____

_____

_____

_____

_____

_____

_____

_____

_____

When taking away the individual's right to
themselves the state decides for them
what they are allowed to do in many
instances. The state grants permissions
through licensing which is nothing more

than paying for the right to break a rule or law. A license steals the unalienable rights of an individual and then sells them back to him.

_____
_____
_____
_____
_____
_____
_____
_____
_____

The responsibility of protecting us from threats to our resources has been reversed, since that threat comes mostly from the state; it is an act of war against citizens. If a government official is in place for our protection and well being why do they steal from us for their survival?

_____
_____
_____
_____
_____
_____

_____

_____

_____

The state unilaterally determines what is theirs through use of force. Taxation is theft because it is taking resources that don't belong to one person by force or with a threat for use somewhere else. Eminent domain is the word for taking what otherwise belongs to a citizen and using it how the state sees fit, even selling it. War is how the state obtains many of the things they call theirs as well.

_____

_____

_____

_____

_____

_____

_____

_____

_____

Even now the government makes war on foreign nations without our consent and for their own purposes; even now they have soldiers ready to take a stand against citizens, arming local law enforcements and training them to subdue any threats to the regime.

_____
_____
_____
_____
_____
_____
_____
_____
_____

The state has asked for loyalty for their causes to the point of death, enlisting young men under ideals they would not surely die for but only kill for, or have others kill for. These men then act out against their own people on their own soil in order to collect revenue to support a system that most are weary of.

_____
_____
_____
_____
_____
_____
_____

_____
_____

Riots have occurred on our own streets,
and false flag attacks have brought
threats of foreigners to our doorsteps,
this kingdom is a war like kingdom and
the leaders have violated our rights with
aggression against us, of which we have a
duty to respond.

_____
_____
_____
_____
_____
_____
_____
_____
_____

Is that a sufficient contract? Is it
one that we can agree sounds eerily
similar in context to the original only
applicable today? Did you find any
personal evidences or communal
evidences that I left out? I am sure
there are plenty of points that I have

missed or not been thorough in describing. Whatever the case may be I present it as a tool to use and consider when you look upon the world that was and the world we currently enjoy. I reason correctly in saying that the drafters of the constitution would not have believed that we would take that document at its word and simply allow ourselves to neglect it at the same time. Better off to allow the whole thing to burn and begin again than to let ourselves repeat the same mistakes.

You can take my version and do with it what you will, alter it, adjust it, add to it, use it... but use it only if you are prepared to replace the current system with one that allows for all that this book describes. If there are small points that you do not agree with, contact me and we can together to work out the details. After all, no words, no thoughts, no ideas can have value... unless people are willing to use those ideas for some good in the world they are a part of.

ECONOMICS

Economics are the nuts and bolts of a free state. It is the desire of the left to take the economy out of the equation giving government full power over the economic future of people. It is the desire of the far left to completely shed themselves of all property, all ownership, all business and commerce. This is the flag that the lazy will crowd under and in it we like to think they will accomplish very little. Beware, beware of the communal purse. At first it seems like hope and love, but it breeds dependence and then want. As for the looter who inevitably comes to take what they believe all men have a right to; not the least of which their rabble, beware of him most of all. He has energy enough to steal and pillage; but lacks the forethought to plant, build, create, and patiently wait. He believes that all resources already belong to him, even if he has not participated in the work... the loot is work enough. He does not reason that someone can own the result of their efforts at all; even though he speaks often of the working class and all of the production.

The only economic paradigm a free state can adhere to is one of total liberty. This means that individuals are left to themselves to trade amongst one another how they see fit and what they desire to trade. This freedom is not a license to violate the freedoms of others. This is the very point; liberty, that exists for the sake of all and not merely a few.

There should be no restriction on trade meaning that there are no guidelines controlling the products available and limit on how people are allowed to trade what they freely own or produce in a manner that does not violate the freedom of others. There are no public restrictions or taxes that are entered into in an involuntary fashion. If an individual or business determines they are willing to submit to a tax from any other person or collection of people for a service of any kind, that contract for those taxes must be entered into without the use of force or coercion.

There are no rules as to the types of businesses permitted and there are no rules as to the types of people or collections of people permitted to own, operate, or create them. All of this is balanced against the key principle that no action from an individual or collection of individuals can limit, reduce, or remove the freedom of another individual in any way. The old axiom, "Your rights end where my rights begin" is upheld as a standard for principles in free society. This will be defined more thoroughly in the following chapter but for the time being just recognize that the subjectivity of rights needs to be reduced to a manageable point that citizens can agree upon. We hear so much about the social contract this day and age and it is my desire to actually establish a social contract that individuals do consent to at the age of citizenship as we earlier described it. Of course this contract is for now an ideal that needs to be refined and offered to individuals rather than forced upon them. For those who do not assent to the contract there is no penalty but at least an awareness that violating the rights of those who assent will be dealt with in a just manner by the just principles described.

Economically we have two major constructs, Micro and Macro. microeconomics is said to be concerned with individuals, their production, and the rules that are in play. Macroeconomics is adversely concerned with the production and economic standards of a nation as a whole. It is in macroeconomics that governments tend to manipulate and change the rules of the game. They invent rules that are passed onto individuals either directly or by effect which are meant to altar the natural movements the market might take. If you consider any of the offices that government is concerned with you recognize a social purpose for their economic response.

Take education as an example; this is generally a state determination and under the authority of districts but applied through federal coercion and bribery. Parents are not simply compelled to supply some form of education, predominately through public resources, it also doesn't matter a bit if they choose an alternative. If a parent can afford a private institute of their choosing they are STILL forced to pay for the public sector and this force may include the funding of principles that the individual finds harmful to the community they are a part of. Furthermore, they are not permitted to receive any of that funding on behalf of their own children for their particular education. It is virtually the same with children that are home schooled. Possibly the worst part of the entire situation is that the individual without children, who may never have children, is ALSO forced to pay for the education of other people's children. It is obviously ridiculous and yet accepted as policy year after year.

So the microeconomic paradigm shows an individual who wishes to home school a child, send a child to public school, or send them to private school; a cost is involved with every choice which has an economic effect on the individual family but that is the limit of the choice. The macroeconomic paradigm is that children MUST be educated to a certain point and therefore we MUST provide this to everyone, even those who could not otherwise pay for it. So that's the economic adjustment, we have to FORCE everyone to pay into a program because we cannot otherwise see how our society would be educated without forcing everyone to participate. It costs us something but what we gain is an educated society. Certainly that last line is very debatable by most conscious citizens.

An Ancap approach to education is one that is less concerned with attempting to manipulate the macroeconomic atmosphere by altering how the society spends its resources involuntarily. We contend that individual rights are MORE important than the perceived rights of who might suffer if we didn't force participation in our programs.

Do schools cease fundraising efforts because of the free money the state gives? Certainly not, but less parents participate in the fundraisers simply because they know they have been paying into the program already. This means that little Johnny gets less money for the projects that his community has interest in because the school has determined it is not as necessary as perhaps him and his peers believe it to be. Luckily plenty of these programs do get funding from donations and fundraisers but how much more would the average program receive if the people being asked were not already being forced to pay?

Most of the time we would see an organic economic atmosphere rise out of the school as children and educators become more creative in ways to fund the programs that they want the most. While at the same time parents and community members can decide to fund, what to fund, and how much to give, based on their concern or interest in the projects as well. We want prosperous communities and kids, why would we choose to withhold resources that we can give for that cause? What's even more compelling is the effort that the children have to put in, in order to obtain what they desire. This is far more educational and necessary for a successful macroeconomic environment then training up children who rely on the system to provide them what they want through no real effort of their own but a sign-up sheet. Some things will come easier than others in life but the public school system gives things freely and scratches their heads at a society that simply expects these things and even takes them all for granted. The entitled children syndrome that is becoming an epidemic is a direct result of the ease at which things are obtained resulting in a lack of value placed on them.

Healthcare is another hot button economic issue that is manipulated by governments for the sake of social construction. The rising cost of healthcare has not been on par with inflation or other economic factors it is the result of government intrusions. One example is forcing the medical industry to carry insurances which force them to raise the cost of their products causing the individual to require insurance in order to afford care. When the medical industry saw this their costs went higher and higher because they didn't have to concern themselves about losing a patient due to cost... someone else paid it and the patient didn't even think about returning to that pharmacy or doctor based on the cost. In walks an uninsured patient and the cost for care has become so high as a result of this game being played out for years; that they cannot do anything but receive the medical care and default on paying. This drives the cost up even higher making up for that default so insurance companies drive their prices up to accommodate the cost. This process repeats itself so much that a $5 shot is sold for $1000 in the U.S. This insanity is then viewed by a frustrated society and the government comes to the rescue. "Everyone needs health insurance, we just force that on the public and there will be no problem." So then the person who doesn't need health insurance because they take care of themselves is still forced to carry it. At the same time the man who couldn't really afford insurance is forced to either sign up for it or pays a penalty. (If you can't afford the insurance how can you afford the penalty?) If you are in the deep poverty

71

zone you get healthcare for free and that is all charged back to the taxpayer.

We have seen that the concept of insurance companies paying for costs has made the price of the products go up. Do you think that the price of the product will go up or down now that the government has determined tax payers will pay for it? The medical industry is a business; they are paying plenty for insurance so they charge that money back on their bill. They also pay plenty in taxes... don't you think they will charge that back as well? Since their taxes are going up to pay for all the new citizens that will be provided for, how do they make up for that loss? You get it yet? They will charge more... and the price hikes continue.

An Ancap approach to healthcare has nothing to do with forcing either doctors or citizens to carry insurance. They are left to themselves. If a doctor wants insurance he can carry it and since it is not forced the cost will lower due to competition in that market. If a doctor opts out of insurance, he is still liable for any harm he causes. If he is a bad practitioner he will not have customers for long. If he is a good one, he will be sought after and thrive. He will only be allowed to charge what the customer is able and willing to pay and he will have fair competition in that area, driving the costs down. (By allowed I don't mean anyone is forcing this, it is a free market standard that you can only survive if you're profiting and you can only profit if you have customers who can pay you.)

As for the man who still cannot afford healthcare, there are free market solutions to government interventions. Non-profit organizations are designed on the principle that they serve a need with their efforts. It is a misunderstanding to assume that people don't get a salary or a paycheck, that's not profit it is cost. It is simply that the profits are used to fund things which groups find important. This non-profit concept encourages people to spend their money on the products produced or even to give donations because they care about that cause. If the need exists someone can find a way to not only meet it but to provide employment while doing so. This is the beauty of the free market. When you limit what a free market is allowed to do you also limit what it is capable of doing.

The solutions to all of the problems society faces economically are not found through forcing social construct, they are available through the economic model itself. That economic model is one of a free market. I can easily come up with solutions just thinking for a short time about each subject and I am not extraordinary, many will come up with better ideas even more quickly. It will take lifetimes to solve new problems that arrive but ultimately allowing people the freedoms they were born with is a noble enough venture.

The economy is not merely about the trade itself it is also about the monetary units utilized. Any unit of exchange is permissible in a free society. If a currency is privately created and people choose to utilize it they may. If a currently known currency is accepted, it must not be forced on any person or business but only accepted voluntarily. If barter is preferred then barter it shall be and no one is stuck trading any single currency. Which is not to say that a single currency might not end up being predominate in the environment; it merely continues to remain a currency of choice and not force.

Banking has become a critical force dominating people's lives, pulling the power on negative banking practices is as simple as loosening restrictions on the markets. It is the crooked governments who force us to follow rules in a rigged game that have caused all of the financial crises in our societies. The current banking system lends money at interest which has no actual value; an Ancap system with free market competition will force banks to secure currencies with actual values in order to obtain customers who will risk, or bother using them. Currently banks simply lend as much as they want in the fractional reserve system having no concern of failure because of bailouts from the fed. An Ancap philosophy will treat that bank like any other business; it only survives if it can.

The entire concept will come down to what a business is willing to trade for and with; if banks cannot control that resource in some way they will be unimportant to businesses and individuals. Properties, production, resources, energy, labor forces, and so on; will become units of value that back monetary units. This is perhaps merely my theory but in a society that can utilize anything available we must recall that there are only a few really valuable resources and the rest is simply serving some comfort which changes so often that we cannot think it to contain enough energy to support a monetary supply chain.

Economic uncertainty is not a liability but an advantage; one will not suppose if the market is safe, they will have a clear responsibility in researching and being assured if it is safe. In other words if you trade a coin that is backed by oil supply you will be responsible for knowing if oil is a viable and necessary resource and how it matches up against the value of corn for instance. There will be plenty of companies who monitor and define these values but you must be cable of making conscious decisions about what you trust. Some trust gold, some trust food, some trust property and an exchange can exist for all of this. In fact, the owner of a coin that claims to back some amount of gold must be exchangeable for that product to the degree that the creator claims it does.

If a monetary unit is backed by construction labor unions then the owner of that unit has the right to call in that value in the form of construction labor that he requires. It is an exciting business model if you entertain the concept long enough. If I trade 100 gold backed coins for 200 labor coins perhaps I can have a building erected by actually going to the creditor and hiring their labor on those coins they distributed. Or I could trade those coins to someone willing to help with my projects. You are free to do what you want without fear of breaking a rule, or law in these economic processes. Virtually any industry can create a valuable currency based explicitly on the value of their products, production capability, services, or resources. There will no doubt be some standard arrived at that classifies this value and supplies access to it directly while lending it to individuals at certain rates that can be agreed upon.

There is One Law

The Law

There has been no law created that stops evil men from doing evil; and there has been no government created that have not perpetrated evil toward its citizens or otherwise. Individuals can only mitigate evil in their life, first through education and second through defense. Understanding the one law is part of the education, defending against violators is putting it into action.

The one law is quite simple but I will expand upon it for the sake of clarity, **"Do not infringe on the liberty of another."** This is pretty straight forward until people begin to bend and twist the definition of liberty. That can be a pretty subjective concept in some circles. One person might suggest it is their right to own child sex slaves. This is of course very ridiculous since the notion itself creates a victim. In the case of the child they are (to most reasonable beings) a very clear victim. As for adults who choose such behavior it becomes tricky because an adult might willingly become a slave. In that case personal morality has to be set aside for the sake of

78

freedom. The "Slave" is not a slave in the strict definition because although they can consent to such behavior they cannot be forced to consent to it or be forced to continue in it. If someone is a willing victim, that is different than a willing participant, who becomes an unwilling victim. More of these details will be considered when we take a look at the NAP [Non Aggression Principle] but for the sake of our understanding let's assume that even seemingly simple concepts will come on the wings of critical scenarios that test the limits of decency. I am not personally an amoral individual, I believe in a creator that has made us in His image and in that system there are clear morals that I make an effort to adhere to. Since I was created with the sovereignty to deny my creator, choose something besides His moral authority, and even choose to set myself at odds with Him; I cannot imagine even the validity of a society that does not also allow for these freedoms regardless of what I believe the result of those choices are.

There are consequences to our actions that we have to live with and sometimes those natural consequences are all that is necessary to annihilate bad behavior without the use of force. For

79

example our current system will continually save the life of an overdosing drug user which might be a noble thing until you recognize that this is paid for with public funds most of the time. On the other hand if someone continually chooses to do drugs they are risking their life in that action and are responsible for their own death if they choose not to alter their behavior. They might die, if they can pay for the life saving efforts they should be made to do just that. If they choose not to pay for these efforts they take their life into their own hands. This is the same with all dangerous activity I suspect; we need to be honest with the risks that we take and not assume that it is someone else's responsibility. What difference does it make to me if someone chooses not to wear a seat belt? I have virtually no concern about this, the belts are available if you would like them but creating a law to make you wear them is a total violation to your freedom.

The same goes for actions that "could" result in the harm of someone else. If they do not result in harm they should not be considered criminal. It is a terrible thing that people are still getting drunk and driving around and the behavior should be discouraged,

80

people need to be educated continually on making better decisions. If someone under the influence of drugs or alcohol gets in a car, drives it, and causes harm to people or property they have violated the rights of those other people and are now liable to provide just recourse and restitution. Sometimes a person dies and in that case equal force might be applicable or at least some form of retribution for family and friends. None of that will bring the person back but creative solutions to stop such violations must be spearheaded. Will we stop them? This is unlikely; but no law has been made that has.

Keep in mind that there have been no laws made that have stopped any crime from being committed. We certainly cannot assume that atrocities in society will cease if we drastically reduce those laws. We can be certain that crime will be reduced because we can stop calling victimless acts crimes. By doing this you will actually stop crime in two ways; those acts no longer being criminal and those people will be less likely to become criminals with victims because they have no need to be trying to get away with anything. Much of the crime that has victims is a result of victimless crimes being protected.

Consider a criminal syndicate that exists to supply narcotics to citizens who want them; generally they will also require all sorts of protection from attacks by the police and law enforcement. They will not only defend their business with force, they have been known to kill people they suspect as undercover agents. The entire atmosphere has become extremely violent in some places simply because the industry is lucrative and people will go to extreme limits to protect it. Consequently we create victims where there wouldn't have otherwise been any.

Remember that Anarchy is not about having no laws; it is about having no masters and no rulers. Enforcing laws becomes a public and private matter and not a power reserved for governments who falsely claim a monopoly on force. A judicial system is an important aspect in an Ancap society. Monetizing that system and granting it authority through agreements made in districts. There can be room for some interpretations of liberties so long as those are voluntarily agreed upon interpretations. Reminding citizens and districts that; *There is one law, "Do not*

infringe on the liberties of another."
helps in reducing the need or
temptation to increase the length and
width of those actions that we currently
call criminal.

The age old struggle between
power and control will continue to some
extent as individuals challenge the range
of contracts and agreements previously
created. I do not suppose that every
scenario presented could be solved
easily through private ownership law and
property rights but they can certainly be
solved as effectively and generally more
effectively than the current system of
courts and judges. As it stands today a
man can hardly fathom representing
himself in any court; it is said that he has
a fool for a client. Under voluntary
systems there are no such things as state
prosecuting attorneys who bring
accusation, experience, and power;
which intimidates and constricts. There
are no arguments based upon what is
allowed to be said and what must be
upheld. There are no, "Objection your
honor" and "Sustained" or "Overruled".
Who can overrule the words and
thoughts? There are only those who
keep order as the parties involved air
out their grievance amongst peers who
they are willing to receive direction

from concerning how to proceed. Will one be compelled to agree and another be rewarded? More than likely and enforcement of these agreements will be as effective as the system designed, no more and no less.

If you assume that I am laying out a legal system for a district, region, or town; then you miss the point. I am merely suggesting that men are their own governors and rulers accountable for what they do toward other governors and rulers. They are fully capable of forming whatever system of governments they choose within their home so long as all participants are in agreement with the system's authority and reach. There is no right or authority inherently granted to a district, region, company, union, collective, or otherwise; that can force anyone to fall under their rule. The reach lasts only as long as the individuals allow it and to the extent that they permit it. As soon as someone reaches to take the liberty of another, they are no longer acting as a free agent but attempting to become a master and it is the right of every free agent to stop that control from overtaking them.

No Masters, No Rulers

How do you then protect the liberty of free agents? How do you stop despotic regimes from simply taking liberty from them because they are stronger or more intelligent? I suspect that in some cases you cannot. The ideals of the liberty minded individual are not accepted by all, they are denied and tossed out the window by those who truly wish to rule by force or make people do things their way. Ancapistan is not an assurance that evil men won't do evil things, but no country has been. The greatest evils we have known have come at the hands of governments and regimes and the only force strong enough to combat it are those who desperately refuse to be ruled at all.

If it is agreed in society that the greatest harm is from governments who wish to rule men than those men will not pledge their allegiance to any government, they will limit the temptation to form classes and groups whose sole purpose is to control and take by force. Those who make attempts at this will generally be run out of town on rails by the people who are accustomed to their freedom and unwilling to submit to authority.

Will some still become victims of small and even despotic governments? Look at our world today, large despotic governments are ruling and controlling people's lives; virtually every aspect of their lives in many examples. Other governments go invade these countries and try to teach the people with force that there is a better way to live, the people do not often learn this; they merely trade one leader for another and the same things occur. It is because they are taught that force is necessary to create and uphold principle and not only force but force in the hands of a small group of protectors. Those invading countries do not help in any real way they have ulterior motives and they become part of the problem rather than the solution. The laws that they have imposed upon their people and the people they invade do not increase liberty and freedom they keep them under coercion and force, sometimes merely at the hand of new masters. That new master might be better and might be worse but it is a master.

We are attempting to throw off the master, to throw off the ruler, to organize ourselves under a concept that can and must do this very thing. The one law is not a model for a government meant to build extenuating laws and guidelines from, it is the one principle point meant to shed the need for masters and rulers at all.

From the brain we have this wonderful place that we call The Mind. Most people will place some willing controls on the mind for the sake of some benefit or another. The mind itself begins from a place of total and absolute liberty. You can think virtually anything that you want at nearly any time. People get lost in their thoughts all of the time when they might have been better off paying attention to something else. Sometimes they recognize this and train themselves to go in a more beneficial direction as far as their thinking... other times they might not.

No one actually has a monopoly on thought, no government has been able to stop it, and not even a single religion has been able to own it... thoughts abound and they continue to occur. Many have tried to control the thoughts of others to varying degrees of success. Some people might willingly allow their thoughts to be controlled in a situation where others would absolutely not. Regardless, the continued power generally exists only as far as that person who has been controlled; chooses to exert some force against this control and ultimately make up their own mind. Most of the time, mind control comes down to very subtle psychological factors that people begin to agree with and adhere to. This is how a government keeps control over a people; they give you comforts and choices to satiate your desire for both of these things.

Comfort and choice are the two most powerful tools that an entity can offer you. They give you perceived happiness and perceived control. If you are provided resources you might otherwise have to work long and hard to procure you may be happy to take them from a group that freely or for only a very small cost offers them. To keep from arousing any suspicion that those offering this comfort or resource are up to no good they give you certain authorities over mostly meaningless and weightless decisions that help you feel as if you are really making an impact on the total operation. So the state gives employment, welfare, and infrastructure. While offering Opportunity to vote on this or that and the ability to write your congressman. For that they force you to pay taxes and follow whatever rules they create but that is mostly just the proverbial man behind the curtain that we don't generally discuss... after all you have roads and the right to vote, why concern yourself with matters of law and finance?

This mind control is threaded so very deep within the society that the Anarchists who it began with hand over their freedom to the state because they believe that the state gave them freedom. Say it another way, "Free men give up freedom in order to be free." You already are free when you are born and your mind is absolute proof of this. Your mind is only chaotic if there is something wrong with it, otherwise it has learned to adhere to the controls YOU put over it because YOU were not interested in chaos. This is virtually the same thing every person has done who is not insane. They only cease being free, cease being the Anarchists they were born as, once they offer that control to someone else.

Now days that free thinker becomes a slave to a government he cannot opt out of. He might be told flippantly that he should leave if he doesn't like the laws. Where should he go? Why should he go? Why is his life, less valuable in the place he is, might even have been born in, simply because a group of people are claiming authority over it? If a person is intentionally harming others and their liberty than I suspect he should be acted against by those he is harming but his mere existence is no less and no more deserving of freedom than anyone else.

In fact we can take this much further. It is not the one who wants the freedom who is the aggressor it is the one taking it. If someone walks up to you and tells you that you are no longer allowed to think about yellow balloons, what is the very next thing you begin to think about? You might agree with them and say that you are not going to think about yellow balloons ever again but I am going out on a limb here and telling you that most will not think less about yellow balloons... but more. In fact, the ones who are thinking the MOST about yellow balloons are the ones telling others not to think about them. Those people are totally focused on yellow balloons and stopping people from thinking about them all day and because of that they are violating their own creed. Doing so makes them a hypocrite even if they justify this by saying, "I must think about yellow balloons in order to do the good work of stopping people from thinking about them." Because the mind is FREE he can't actually stop a single being from thinking about yellow balloons who doesn't simply decide to do so; on his own. Yet by force he might still stop people from openly talking about them. He might stop people from selling them. He might stop the balloons from existing in that society... he might... but he will not stop the thoughts and so long as those exist... the yellow balloon is only a few moments out of reach for all men.

Your liberty is a yellow balloon; one you were born to look upon, consider, and even experience. You have masters telling you not to look at them, hold them, own them, or think about them. They don't come out and tell you not to any more, they don't snatch them out of your hand as often as they used to, they merely hand you a red balloon and tell you that it is the same or better in some way. You have a choice now. That choice for the yellow balloon might be available but that red balloon is lifted up as a savior... a great protector. That red balloon comes with all sorts of "free" and wonderful gifts but you cannot keep the yellow balloon. You have to eradicate or altar your ideas about liberty. You can't have your roads and your education with the yellow balloon... only the red one. They use coercion, "Your dear sick mother... what would she do without all that the red balloon has provided... and you want to abandon that for this yellow balloon that would make her pay for her own medical care?" They convince you that your desire for liberty is selfish all while they are taking from you and others who don't wish to give. They don't even see the selfish nature of such behavior to take what is not theirs. They ask you again, "Would you rather see your dear Mother suffer?" Convinced, you might let go of that yellow balloon... that liberty; take on that master who will save you and hold that red balloon over your head. When this occurs you will have to believe that you made the correct choice, you will have to believe that you are doing the right thing and you will begin to force this upon others in a similar fashion.

Who among us would allow their Mother to suffer? I can tell you... the state. The ones who sell themselves to you as the protectors and saviors are the same ones who will turn against you and destroy you as soon as you can't follow through with orders and compliance. Who among us would not protect our Mothers? We do not lose the power to help our loved ones when we gain the liberty of self ownership. We gain access to the tools to do something and to people who know what it is like to lose loved ones. Freedom does not change any of that... it is a tactic used to gain support through emotion because the system itself makes no logical sense.

If your mind cannot allow you to let mankind suffer, why would your hands stop you from helping them? Why do you assume that a magical organization calling themselves: GOVERNMENT is the only way or has the only strength needed to stop this suffering? It is because they tell you this, and they tell you this because they need you to continue to accept that the red balloon is better than the yellow one, that the control is better than the liberty, and that the master is necessary for any freedom. Even though the master is the contradiction to the freedom they propose they are offering.

What I am really trying to say, is that you are already free. Your mind can think all about the yellow balloon regardless of who says you cannot or should not. You are also free to think all about red balloons, or blue, or any other color you choose. You are free already and no one can take that freedom of thought; even if they try. You have to give it away FREELY. Your freedom stops as soon as you attempt to force others to think about or not think about any color balloon they choose. So Anarchy already exists and its limits only go so far as to their effect on the next person. When someone begins to force people to think of one over the other or to not think about one at all, they are attempting to control and master those people and are no longer acting as an agent that considers liberty important.

This is so easy to see in the realm of thoughts. People might not like the thoughts of others but the only ones who act with force are those who merely want to control. Someone recently attempted to explain to me that Anarchy means that people are free to use violence. No that is actually a contradiction. Anarchy means no masters and no rulers. If someone attempts to use violence against another they are essentially trying to master and rule them and they cease to be an anarchist... they are a despot.

Restrictions are Mutual

Any restriction put upon an individual in any way must be mutually agreed upon by those it restricts. We have established that use of force is despotism at its root and so use of force to create restrictions on people is the same as force, it is where states begin. In other words, if you tell someone they will get punched in the face for wearing a shirt with a yellow balloon you are beginning to force restrictions on people. You are fully allowed to make statements such as this but you are not free to follow through. If you merely tell someone to do this or that, you're in the clear but if you use force to restrict them you are not.

If the person is willing to move forward with wearing the yellow balloon shirt and they get punched, the aggressor is in violation of the rights of that citizen and they are in effect no longer a free agent, they have become a despotic ruler and should be dealt with as such. That violation can be responded to with the use of equal or greater force deemed necessary at the time by the person acted upon or the parties who witnessed the action. It doesn't matter so much what the reason for the use of initiated force was it is the force itself. If someone puts a gun to your head and tells you to take off the yellow shirt or die, you surely do not have to wait for death in order to respond. The restriction, the command, the first act of force is contained in that threat and is in fact a viable enough use of force for the one being restricted to respond with equal or greater force.

This is all about property rights. You have a right to yourself, whatever you produce, whatever you obtain through mutual exchange, and whatever you choose to do so long as that does not infringe on the liberty of others. If someone suggests that you are infringing on their liberty by wearing a shirt that offends them you have to consider this. Did you violate his property? In other words is he or his property altered in some way that it requires restitution? He might argue that there are mental damages and it sounds like there are...

they just are not the result of the shirt being worn or anything that you have done merely by choosing to wear a shirt that he did not like. On the other hand, attacking you for wearing it; that is a clear violation of your property... no matter what the excuse for the attack might be.

Rothbard in "For a New Liberty" uses a wonderful example of property rights verses the right to free speech. He tells of a character that stands up in a theatre and yells during the movie. The left uses this as an example to suggest that free speech has limits, a man can't go ahead and disturb others in such a way, we have to limit the extent of free speech and where it is allowed. Rothbard reminds us that it is not an issue of free speech it is an issue of property rights. If the man is the theatre owner he might think he has some right to behave in this way. In fact he might but not if he had led the customers to believe they would be watching a film in peace. They would be defrauded and he would be guilty of violating their property rights based on the tickets they purchased. In similar fashion if the disturbance came from a patron, he has not only violated the property of the other patrons but he has violated the property of the business owner who no doubt will not put up with such outbursts.

In the more common areas of day to day life we might believe that it will be harder to define freedoms as people go out and bounce off one another sometimes even crossing the lines of property rights and the liberty of others. If the outbursts of free speech can be shown to negatively impact the freedoms of others than a clear agreement as to who violated whose rights can be obtained. I am sure that there will be disputes that are not easily solved through simple scenarios that we ponder now or ever. I am also sure that we cannot suppose that it is possible to balance the scales of life through any social constructions that limit freedoms.

There will be occasions where the inequalities of life reveal that one man owns more than another. That one citizen can produce better quality goods or services than another. Some people are merely stronger or more intelligent than others. Should we lower the bar socially? Should we decrease the potential of the entire society so that a few might have that extra boost to get where they believe they ought to be or where others believe they ought to be? How about that man who works harder and gains advantage, should his production be offered up without his consent for this cause making him the producer of less than his best because others are in need?

In Ancapistan we do not suggest that no one might help the less fortunate we merely suggest that no one can force it. It is certainly not charitable for you to lobby that your government take more from its citizens for the sake of what you find important. For goodness sake if you find it important leave that man alone who you are attempting to force his goods and services from and go provide yourself for whatever purpose you deem important.

Whatever is holding you back is the same sort of stuff that was holding everyone back who solved those problems. One might be stronger or smarter but they certainly didn't get that way by concerning themselves with comparisons. People grow for one reason and one reason alone they have a will in them to do so.

Personal responsibility is an important character trait for anyone to be successful in anything they attempt which is true regardless of the political and economic atmosphere. We must remember that an attempt to even the playing field by either limiting what someone is allowed to do or taking from their resources without permission; actually tilts the playing field favoring the less capable. There is only one way that we can view equality and it is in our approach to allowing people the liberty they were born with, as soon as you attempt to quell that liberty you are crushing your own liberty as well.

AGGRESSION, FORCE, COERCION

NAP stands for the Non Aggression Principle. I am sure most of my readers know that already. It may also be referred to as the Non Aggression Axiom but that doesn't produce the same pleasing acronym. It is basically the philosophy that aggression is illegitimate. Of course it is not pacifism so much as it is the idea that the **initiation** of force is illegitimate. If someone initiates aggression, force, or coercion they are acting in an unacceptable manner and the use of force against them is legitimate.

Individuals have an inherent right to protect their property and at times the property of others. They can defend people who want or require defense against anyone that is being subjected to a NAP violation. A NAP violation should be somewhat obvious in this context, is there a victim? This cannot be stressed enough, you see we have The One Law and within that framework the reality of the NAP is exposed but it is actually the NAP which defines the extent of that one law. Infringement upon liberty is a NAP violation; it is taken down to its core. "Do not infringe on the liberty of another," can certainly be applied to individuals but as a societal construct it is meant to deter groups from forming against individuals for any purpose, and it is meant to help you recognize when any individual or group is attempting to rule you. As people interact with one another it is much easier to look at things from the point of individual aggression. They are in effect defining one another but zeroing in on separate areas of focus within a larger environment. Regardless, initiation of force is the first step toward state control. The one law is the first and last requirement of a free state. The NAP is the principle that actually guides that law.

Governments do not follow a principle of non aggression; they enforce edicts with aggression before they ever respond to a single aggressive act. This is why the NAP is not an edict that can be set up with clear plans for enforcing it in each scenario. Those definitions and descriptions would create a plethora of rabbit holes that would become as overbearing as our current system of laws and governance. The NAP is the guideline for dealing with things in a civilized manner. We cannot force our personal morality on men. Morality is the very best that a person can decide for themselves, the NAP is the very least. At the very best I will honor everyone, be polite, and accommodating. At the very least I will not use aggression, force, or coercion against someone unprovoked.

This is certainly not the framework for a system of government in that it would be insufficient in that aim and contradictory to our cause. It is actually a way to keep individuals from acting like governments act toward others and therefore forming factions that act in that way. The whole point being that we don't really need a small group of people to tell us what we ought to do and ought not to do; we merely need to agree that we shouldn't be aggressive toward others. Ancapistan is not an ideal that requires some form of governance; its governance is exclusive to individuals who accept some portion of that ideology. You govern yourself because you own yourself.

There are boundaries in place, both in nature, and among people who interact with one another. Those boundaries are determined by some experience that a collection of people have, for example; the NAP is a valid boundary that both allows for freedom and protects freedom.

SUBJECTIVITY

Often people will get lost under
the subjective nature of the NAP.
People will argue endlessly about its
interpretation. Those arguments
generally come from people who either
don't want to believe such a thing is
possible or merely want to destroy the
personal liberties of others.

There are too many occasions
and scenarios concerning what a NAP
violation is and is not for us to even
consider being able to fully define
them. This always comes back to what a
victim actually is and is not. Some may
claim to be a victim when no tangible
harm has occurred against their person
or property. Others will claim they are
victimizing no one when in fact they have
a trail of injured people and properties.
It is not possible to throw a blanket
over the whole of humanity in order to
comfort them; you will in fact suffocate
many of them. This is why Ancapistan is
such a wonderful concept, we will
acknowledge problems and we will go to

work solving them without the use of force and coercion.

We will remain subjective with the situations and therefore avoid being locked down to the same principle that police and military have used to justify terrible actions, "I was just following orders." That's not really a viable excuse for violating someone else. Governments decide who can be held accountable and they give their agents a free pass. In a society where citizens are utilizing the NAP as a gauge for offence the subjectivity is actually a good thing, recognizing that every situation is different allows for a different response based upon the actually situation and not some variation in history. We can certainly refer to a variation but not as a blanket for decision making.

A lot of this comes down to determining who will or can enforce such decisions. Of course there are times when the individual is the only one present and a decision must be made; especially in a life or death situation. If harm was done than their will no doubt be a victim and that victim might retaliate in some way or his loved ones might. This is bound to occur time to time whether you live in an anarchist society or one that is ruled by a totalitarian government... these things occur among humans as a form of their nature. This is not to say that groups cannot work with private arbitration companies who mitigate the decision making process by supplying a viable solution. Certainly religious groups who people choose to be a part of can solve troubles that arise out of members of their religious order and that is expected. All of this has to be understood through the lens of the NAP because perceived violations can certainly bring people to the defense of themselves or a group.

This is a pretty laissez faire (live and let live) attitude, not one that is designed to do the opposite; kill and let kill. Those acting in such a way will certainly be acted against by people who will not tolerate the destruction of liberty. That collection may be called a government in the minds of some people but they are not rulers and they cannot and will not take funding involuntarily from anyone. So it is left for the market to work out. As it stands today we must recognize that the market has not been free of the government and is therefore not at all free. So any comparison to how the market would destroy rather than help a people is felonious and manufactured through an understanding of capitalism that survives because of government not independent of the government. Since capitalism in its raw form finds the easiest most efficient way to success possible; it utilizes governments to get there in societies that are not free.

A free market capitalist society is a different thing, having no public entity to suck from it must malign itself with the people who control it. This means that it must exist for the people and by the people only in exactly the same way that the government of some countries has attempted to exist. In other words it is only capitalism that can live for the people and by the people because capitalism is created BY THE PEOPLE, and only survives if THE PEOPLE ARE THE

CUSTOMERS. When this is a willing and not a forced relationship the teeth that many are afraid capitalism has are actually sawn smooth.

When I say that capitalism will solve all of the social ills of society I am not saying that it may or that it possibly could; I am saying that capitalism is literally the people solving problems in their lives day in and day out. It works on a small scale and even better on a large scale. The only time capitalism becomes the beast we cannot kill is when we are forced to buy rather than compelled by our desire to buy.

In the case of police, we are forced to pay for them and on top of that force they use force against us to both fine us and limit our freedom. In the case of private security and even bounty hunters they exist to solve a problem and are paid to solve that problem, if they do a bad job they are fired... there is no paid vacation... the customer says no and hires someone else. A bounty hunter or private security officer is accountable for their actions independent of the person paying them

109

and can choose to work for the person or not. Unscrupulous people will be weeded out and those the communities choose to use will be the companies that they use.

Problems exist; people will have to set up agreements among one another that I will not attempt to define here but freedom is better than slavery. Currently you are told you are free and you can only look out onto your world from a very limited cage. You can break free from that cage but you MUST be willing to accept the risks that freedom has always carried. Every animal knows that running free is better than being in a cage... but out there in that big world some do not survive. It will always be this way and the only question is do you want the ILLUSION of safety to restrict your freedoms?

CONTRACT IMPLEMENTATION

This is not something that can be forced upon anyone. Of course there are limits to that statement as well. Private property can be protected from violations against it. This means that if your rules are made clear to people who are then given permission to enter your property they are subject to that contract. If someone enters your property uninvited they are also subject to your rules because they are on your property and did not take the time to know the rules and may not even be welcome on your property. If someone is invited on your property and you have rules that fall outside of the NAP and reasonable understanding of personal rights and you neglect to inform them or simply refuse to then you cannot reasonably expect them to comply. You can still ask them to leave at any time.

Beyond this the contract engagements are pretty straight forward, if you enter into an agreement with someone be sure you understand the terms and that they also have a similar understanding. Many contracts are verbal and simply don't require much. If someone wants to buy a car and you have a car to sell, let the buyer beware as they are even now. If they agree to buy and you agree to sell and you agree on the terms, the contract was made without formal proceedings.

In the case of larger purchases or those with special terms it might be beneficial for those to be formally agreed upon. In today's world a contract is threaded with so much legal nonsense that you need a translator to comprehend it. In Ancapistan this is not the case, there is no reason to overcomplicate because you do not have a state enforced legal system that will make one become bound to something they did not understand. Clarity is the key because the contract you are signing is merely stating that you understand the terms. People will certainly want to understand the terms and companies will also want to sell things... therefore they will need for people to understand.

If a car dealer works with a bank to create a loan and the paperwork is not understood the person had better not sign it until they do because there is no governing body that they can merely ASSUME is protecting them. So they will end up paying closer attention. In the same way the seller will want to be sure that the buyer understands so that they don't end up with a customer who defaults. Both rely on a government to force the other to comply through litigations where as a free society will grant both parties less protection equally creating an environment where personal responsibility is the most important factor.

Some may argue that is a bad thing until they realize how uncluttered their lives will become. You don't understand a contract... don't sign it, because Joe down the road wants your business and he will create a contract you can understand with terms you want. In fact, as many people as there are who fail you in commerce there will be three or four who see this problem and drive them out of business with a willingness to both value you and serve you.

Licensing will not be required for anything that is done. Obviously on private property if someone demands a license of some sort that is a separate matter. There are no licensing boards publicly or people who bother with determining whether a contractor is qualified, that's up to the consumer. There may be licensing companies who teach contractors how to do this or that, which give them some advantage over one who has no seal of quality that is recognized, but a license is not required and therefore anyone can set up a company in any industry and begin to overcome the shortcomings of whatever exists. There should be no fear involved, people will simply have to do better homework concerning those companies they use and reputation management will increase as a viable business. Again it comes down to taking responsibility.

Every transaction in life is a contract of some sort and instead of relying on the government to make decisions for us based on their inability to effectively do anything; we get to make our own decisions and enjoy the fruits of those decisions. There is no doubt in my mind that we will have to accept the consequences of some bad decisions as well; but unlike the social justice warriors, we admit that.

Furthermore, there are bad consequences now, and they are not the result of one single factor; they are the result of multiple failings from one single source... government and the people involved in extending its powers. The only good government official is the one who would do away with the government completely. This is like that good cop bad cop paradigm, there are no good cops; they all work for the broken system and will do its bidding... even to the point of killing citizens. This does not mean that they cannot change, they simply need to renounce their allegiance to that cause and work for the liberation of themselves and their loved ones, in this small way we can all effectively destroy the beasts that governments are.

DECRIMINALIZING FREEDOM

Of course the concept of what a criminal is has been totally skewed by an absurd amount of laws. So much of what people do these days is considered criminal and there are in fact no victims. Without a victim there is absolutely no crime. Sometimes there is no crime when someone calls themselves a victim so how can we live under the assumption that the absence of a victim can still produce a crime? It is absolute madness on a grand scale that we have allowed our legal system to go so far over the edge.

Instead of spending this time trying to focus on how we might deal with those crimes that involve a victim I want to defer to our previous conversation concerning NAP violations and The One Law. This time should be spent talking about those freedoms we now have once the restrictions of the masters and rulers are disposed of. Because we can do virtually anything we want so long as it

116

harms no one or their property; we will no longer have to concern ourselves with permission of any sort. If you want to sell drugs, sell drugs. If you want to make guns, make guns. If you want to be a prostitute, be a prostitute. If you want to sell real estate then by God sell real estate... and GASP... even without a license!

This has not one single thing to do with the morality of what you think is right personally or how you view society. No one will force you to buy drugs, guns, sex, or houses; but whose business is it if someone sells those things to the people who want to buy them? It is merely the business of the people buying and selling them and no one else. It only becomes the business of someone else if a victim of some sort or another is created.

A good example for the failings of government to prevent crime is identity theft. Everyone knows that identity theft is a real problem and there are tough laws combating it. They have no effect on the actual crime. What actually does, have an effect on the crime, is the private security measures being taken by companies to protect their liabilities and their customer's liabilities. The government's involvement is a small part of the tracking systems that private companies are using to crack down on this crime and catch the perpetrators. The government has to defer to private companies for most of the things it does that are considered valuable and yet we still think it is them doing it.

Another good example of government failing is in all forms of vice crime. They cannot stop people from buying and selling these things now, not even a little bit. So what in the world makes us think that we need a government to protect us from these things? The truth is; the taxpayer is the one who ends up paying for these things and why should they? My question is valid, why should taxpayers be supporting criminals especially when the criminals have no victim and were merely trading something they wanted with someone who had it? Furthermore, if you are a victim why should you be forced to again pay for a crime that was committed? For example, a man comes and steals something from you, he is caught and forced to pay restitution. He is then sent to a prison where he gets housing paid for by you and food paid for by you, doesn't that nullify the theft? In many cases no restitution is paid, the man gets your money and then also gets free room and board paid for by you.

I am not suggesting that prison or jail is a wonderful place that these people wish to spend their time; of course they would rather be free [In some cases, Stockholm Syndrome exists; we see it every day in society.] it simply is asinine for the public to be supporting those that it is also punishing. It would be like the demonstrators of the Boston tea party buying their own tea, paying tax for the transaction, and then dumping it in the ocean... oh wait... some other people did something similar in modern times.

The Boston tea party was about not paying taxes on imported products. It was about destroying the king's product before it could be sold with the new tax attached. It was about doing something that was criminal in response to a crime. In the eyes of the American public these men are revolutionary heroes championing the often repeated phrase, "No Taxation without Representation!" The precursor to our modern day, "Taxation Is Theft." In the eyes of the king they are criminals and nothing more, the men involved knew this; that's why they dressed up like Mohawk Indians, and it was the first false flag I guess. Without spending much time on those politics let's just recognize that they understood that they were criminals in the eyes of the king. So why do we pretend as if we are anything else than criminals in the eyes of our rulers?

If you are interested in something as radical as eliminating the state, you are a threat to the state, in other words a criminal. Okay, maybe you're not that radical yet... maybe you simply believe that taxes should be voluntary and no one should coerce you into anything that you don't consent to. This is wonderful and we can work with that... sort of a progressive move toward state eradication; the thing is... you're still an enemy to the cause of the state. If you think for a minute that state is going to consent to allowing you to decide whether or not you pay for a license or any other illegal tax; you are absolutely deluded, they force you now and they will not stop forcing you until enough people throw off the chains and simply make them leave. The people who do that... they are criminals in the mind of the state and that will NEVER change.

Please understand my purpose, it is first to encourage activity to continue which does not result in victims regardless of legality. Second it is to encourage retaliations to force that have been initiated against citizens who would otherwise be willing to live peacefully had they not been bothered with organized mobs attempting to use aggression, force, or coercion against them. Third, it is to remove the authority of the state completely placing it squarely into the hands of citizens to do what they wish so long as they do not violate the liberty of anyone else.

BECOMING FREE

THE FOLLOWING INFORMATION IS EXTREMELY RADICAL, REVOLUTIONARY, AND IN SOME CASES ILLEGAL IF APPLIED

YOU ARE FREE TO ACCEPT THE CONSEQUENCES OF YOUR OWN ACTIONS AND HAVE NO ONE TO BLAME BUT YOURSELF IF THOSE ACTIONS HAVE RESULTS THAT YOU DO NOT LIKE

PLEASE PROCEED WITH EXTREME CAUTION

Freedom means that you simply do what and act how you choose, independent of organized control that you do not consent to. This freedom cannot violate the rights of others as we have repeated multiple times. I will hand you the tools you need to build this kingdom which will inevitably replace all others.

Up to this point we have considered many ideas and I encourage my reader to learn more about freedom. You can find many resources online such as books and free papers that outline thoughts and principles. I only outline a few because my purpose is to put the wheels in motion. To some extent we require trust amongst one another but in the information age we merely need to disseminate ideas and allow the chips to fall where they may. In other words I do not have to incriminate myself by writing a book that tells you how to do these things and at the same time be caught following every aspect of my advice. Such actions would be held against me in their courts of law and I would never see daylight again. I simply wish to put ideas forth that are revolutionary and action based in the hopes that many people read these words and understand them.

If only a few begin to understand them, we shall outrun the legality of our actions and decriminalize our actions. So the goal is to get this book into as many hands as possible, not only to help me and my very legal cohorts build and continue to build the most legal form of this principle we can; but also to allow us to create more material that can help you to build that other side of this philosophy which is desperately required.

So before we go any further I give you a task, disseminate this information far and wide, it will eliminate the ability of the enemy to track who is carrying out what; and it will fund the legal resources you and others might need. It will also fund our underground building company which specializes in off grid homes built partially or completely underground... I don't have to explain why this might be a fun concept.

Let's assume you or someone you know has the resources to buy some property, anywhere... in a city, out in the country, in a rural area. Let's start with property. You want to be sure that the person named on the property as the owner is free of being suspected of any crime or criminal activity. As we proceed we will access background checking programs and things of that sort. There needs to be a database of current law enforcement and government agents that can be used to make certain that people are who they say they are and are not double agents from the state.

Once the property is acquired it is important that a proper security system be installed. Measures need to be taken to debug the home or environment and measures need to be made to watch the home remotely. This can be tricky since an internet feed can be traced but I am sure some computer savvy folks can work on devices we sell that will be known in our communities as being secure. Security is very important. Remember that law enforcement have all day every day to invent ways to trap you in their webs and they are secure in themselves going home and resting peacefully under the belief that what they are doing is for the good of humanity.

You need to take on the same mindset. Your actions need to be impenetrable in that you are 100% secure that what you are doing is good and right, better than what your enemy has been doing. If you cannot arrive at this conclusion perhaps you should not attempt these tasks, merely recognize that the whole idea was a phase and go sell shoes someplace with Mr. Bundy... we all need shoes anyway. I'm joking of course, every aspect of society will be represented in Ancapistan and they are all necessary, so whatever industry you are in and whatever skills you have, build them. Most of what I am going to say on the following pages is intended for those personalities and people who can stomach breaking the law in the same way the early revolutionaries of America could.

If you can arrive at that conclusion then proceed. Be assured now that the location is secured. I would suggest that you find a vehicle that blends in with other vehicles and be very careful to notice if anyone is noticing you. Consciousness is key; paranoia is close behind but you do want to guard against going too far. One method I always used if I believed I was followed was simply to take my tail in a direction off course to where I was headed, this is always easy and usually ends in the realization that no one was actually following... Better safe than sorry.

The next stage for you is to create someone. This is not too difficult, just find some information online and invent someone. Give them a back story, create a persona online. Do not use a device generally used or in a place you might normally work. Once internet is on at the property (If you have it there) feel free to use a device that cannot be traced to you for the purposes of accessing that account and even communicating with yourself. The purpose here is to appease any nosey investigators; being certain that the information does not lead back to you or your devices. You will not need much information, a fake address, fake SSI #, fake name, fake photo. Try to use the photo of someone who is obscure and perhaps not with us anymore. I am sure photo shop can help. You are not stealing someone's identity, I do not advocate this sort of activity, it is frustrating to the poor bastards it effects and since it creates a victim you are violating your own principles. Use an identity that when investigated by police either takes them in circles, nowhere, or to the obvious conclusion that they are fake... but again not traced back to you.

Your purpose here is to offer up a sacrifice, IF and only IF you're property is somehow compromised. In other words, this property is merely an investment property and your straw man is the renter. Put together a rental agreement of some sort, talk to the guy over the phone and online, take down his information, and collect money orders for payment. Other than that you don't know the guy, you don't bother the guy, you don't need to... he is a great tenant, always paying on time with a form of payment that is as good as cash... why would you pry?

This property is your starting point for whatever industry you have in mind. It might be a production facility, a storage point, or a technology space. It could be virtually anything you need it to be. You don't have to worry much about being there from time to time so long as most of the activities are still put away or hidden from the casual observer. You have a key and it's your property and often the tenant is out of town and needs you to repair something. This will allow your fingerprints to be acceptable at the location along with your DNA. The lack of other DNA evidences might arouse their suspicion but again that's not your business, you just thought he was a great customer.

This property can be used for all sorts of wonderful activities, some legal and some considered illegal by the statists that think they own citizens. What you do with and on this property is entirely your business as far as anyone should be concerned. It is really only your business and the business of those you choose to involve. This is not to say that people will not bother you and try to make these things their business. I suggest you stay alert.

One idea that comes to mind is in the area of weapons productions. It is necessary for citizens to be armed in case someone attempts to violate them or their property. The problem is that modern gun ownership is all about gaining permission. Many authoritarians use the excuse that gun access will increase crime rates. Of course that's true in a society that considers having a gun a crime in many instances. When you operate from a place that understands a crime has to include a victim you realize that the guns don't create the victims the people who refuse to respect personal rights do. This person is less concerned about breaking laws than we are... if they are willing to victimize people; don't you think they are also willing to obtain guns at any cost? Either way, we believe it is their liberty to do so... but it is our liberty to shoot them when they try to victimize us. In order to do that we need guns.

Recently I saw a device that costs around $1500 and it is designed to turn a raw AR-15 lower receiver (which is currently legal for anyone to buy in the U.S.) into a usable lower receiver. This technology is exactly the sort of thing needed all over the world in order to even the playing field a bit. As long as no one knows who has guns, and who does not, there can be no monopoly on force. In the hands of the

Ancap this is some of the most important technology they could wield, being able to not only make as many weapons as they desire but to also have the ability to arm whoever they choose to do business with. Be on guard if you plan to sell to people who want to buy, the state will attempt to stop and infiltrate this action with everything they have. We will try and encourage as much of this as possible.

Perhaps that property above is merely used to order these products online and have a drop off point, this alone could bring pesky intruders but it is a starting off point to getting the device onto the street and quickly to an undisclosed location. For a list of some of these devices and products look at https://ghostgunner.net/collections/featured-products

The next side of this organizing is to connect with other people whom you can trust. You have to have an assurance that the people you allow into your life are in fact trustworthy people who you are willing to risk yourself for. Families are good but often family members cannot stay on the same page. You have to be sure that you can trust family members as well. Connecting with a network of people is very important but it must be set up in such a way that you do not expose everyone and everything. This is a leaderless resistance, that's the whole point of Ancapistan, to have no leaders but to still have leadership that you can choose to follow if you see a benefit. If you have four friends that you talk to on a regular basis about your ideas try to keep them apart. Attempt to keep them in secrecy about the things that you and they discuss together. Then encourage them to find people they can trust two or four at a time but tell them you do not wish to know them and do not wish for them to know you. Those friends should be encouraged to deal separately with your friend so that too many people don't know too much about one another.

You can share information about certain things and ideas about other things. Although each of these things can be disseminated to the entire group as

132

it repeats this model, tracing the information back to its source can be tough. If you do end up with a mole they are limited in how far into the organization they can penetrate. They cannot actually penetrate the whole organization because there is in fact no central leader, only bands of independent people doing independent things.

Another interesting tactic to consider, when trying to operate undisturbed, is to emulate law enforcement. This can go as far as you would like it to go so long as you remember that violating the liberty of others is a line that should not be crossed. I would suggest that you look into the types of unmarked vehicles being used by police and make your vehicles look as much like them as you can. This will give the illusion that you are an officer and will automatically build a defense against law enforcement and citizens.

Most of what Ancapistan needs to be focused on is monetary. The capitalism side of this can really shine when you get rid of regulation. We could start all sorts of companies that are unlicensed, teach our teams how to do this and be making money on any of them right away. You fund Ancapistan by putting that money toward properties and infrastructure and even by supporting people like us who are building from a more legal perspective that actually want to be an example of an Ancap nation.

Another purpose is to stop paying taxes when and how we can. Either stop filing all together if possible, or begin to find ways around taxes and the like. If you can hire people and pay them under the table you always should. If you can be paid under the table you always should be. That work you are doing is yours and belongs to no one else and so does your pay. Don't admit anything to anyone about what you make; it's none of their business. On the other hand be sure and invest in things that cannot be easily traced or stolen. I'm no big fan of banks personally although I recognize the need for utilizing them in a limited way. Be careful that you do not get your finances too wrapped up in that scheme or you could lose everything.

While we are on the subject be sure to never answer questions from law enforcement. http://fairdui.org/ has state specific documents that you can save and print for use while driving. Look into other resources that protect free speech in your area and the right to not answer questions at all. Many times you can simply repeat the phrase to officers, "I do not answer questions." The only other thing you need to say is that you would like a lawyer. They are obligated to allow you to speak with a lawyer and if they continue questioning you, most of what you say will be thrown out at trial, of course I would suggest that you say nothing regardless.

Most of this is known these days but the reality is that police still get confessions. They are not your friends, they are not trying to help you out or keep you out of trouble; they exist to get convictions and you need to keep your mouth shut and wait for a lawyer at all times. Never, ever, allow them to search a vehicle or your property without a warrant. If they have probable cause they will search, if they have suspicions they should get a warrant, if they ask permission from you; ALWAYS REFUSE TO GRANT IT.

Currency and banking control the world through government regulation that is anti-capitalist. People who are anti-capitalist generally are confused by the current system. It is the state that controls commerce through their relationships with large banks. Without the state the large banks would have to compete for the business of individuals and the individuals would never be forced to use their products.

It was with this in mind that I discovered a way to capture some of the business that banks and states are stealing from citizens; for use in our communities. If I have a product or service that I want to sell and you want to buy, I can set terms for that product or service that we mutually agree upon. Not only that, I can set standards for customers through contracts that the customer signs. Think of it like wholesale clubs that are only open to members.

The customers in our networks will be able to use our products and services only after they become members. This is not forced, neither by the buyer or seller, it is only a contract that you can agree to or steer clear of. The club would operate on a private currency in which members do not pay cash for products or services they trade the cash for the currency similar to prepaid products and services. These prepaid transactions can occur months before or moments before the actual transaction occurs. The currency is converted into a private monetary system that is electronic for the most part and tradable only amongst members of the cooperative. Amongst one another we trade goods and services but we have no taxable obligations whatsoever.

The goal here is to have a strong enough economic system that people want to trade their currency for ours. The creation of the currency can happen in a number of ways and to begin with it would happen mostly through exchanging one currency for our private currency. It could also occur through private individuals who trade their production for the currency. For example, if the owner of a plumbing company contracts with the bank to provide 30 man hours for $1000 the currency is created and backed by that contract for 30 hours of work. It is the banks responsibility to ensure that such a debtor does not overextend themselves so that when that debt is called due it can be used.

The method for doing this is quite easy; it could begin with any form of business that is now utilized. Vending machines are a good example. If a vending machine company existed that took credit cards, cash, or other forms of currency and traded that for credits on their systems and only took credits from their systems; than offices or locations that have these systems would be effectively converting the currency while profiting from the products sold. The goal here is to capture a market share by offering the products cheaper through these machines than the competition. The only downside to the average Non-member citizen user; is that the currency cannot be exchanged back into the currency that it derived from. It can only be exchanged for a product from the machines.

You would want to create a minimum conversion of say $20 which are equal to 20 credits (for simplicity sake, the actual currency exchange would more than likely change as the value of the credits outran that of the USD) these credits are non refundable, the reason for converting is that the item in the machine might cost say 20% less than the competition. A person using a machine in the area might choose a monthly budget that is more easily controlled. If you spend 100 a month at machines now you might consider using these and budgeting for 80, it is viable and simple.

As the company grows they would want to extend the use of these credits to local companies in the area where the machines are. Consider college campuses. Not only could students get the vending machine items they want at a lower rate through conversion but if local stores and businesses accept the credits this will encourage them to convert more. You will contract with the stores to pay them the value equal to the USD they spend minus a small transaction fee comparable to that of credit card companies. Furthermore if local club stores begin to pop up where no other currency is accepted you will begin to capture more of your local currency.

There are no doubt details that need to be worked out and perhaps huge legal issues that need to be addressed along the way. Such a move would certainly help grow the economic value of Ancapistan among citizens of any town it is utilized. It would be an enormous revenue builder for the cause as well since every unit of trade is automatically accepted before the product sold is even acquired. This sort of cash flow is enormous to building a business quickly and effectively.

There are so many opportunities present that industrious minds could put to work for the sake of building the infrastructure needed for Ancapistan to suddenly exist organically. It is possible that governments will fail people to such a degree that armed men and women will one day violently overthrow them. It is necessary that networks of Ancaps exist to take up the work of offering true solutions for a replacement system. The best replacement system will be one that offers solutions without utilizing coercion and aggression; it is the Ancap alone that does this very thing. We do not need to act because something is legal we need act because it is necessary, and individual freedom is necessary.

LIVING FREE

Living free might only be possible after the existence of a free society, but where do you suppose that society can exist? It is impossible for a truly free society to exist within a larger system that is coercive and aggressive. The best you can do is to create a network of people who want to live as free as they can. You can also consider communal living although many will fear that this is automatically some sort of communist concept. It is really more about leveraging resources to purchase large tracts of lands which are governed only by the residents, so although you might fear that it would devolve into a regime it is likely that if all the individuals involved are simply self owners they will follow that philosophy within their collective neighborhoods.

The entire idea of living free comes down to a mindset about your life. You will begin to be more free if you can recognize both how to allow for the freedom of others and easily see when that freedom is being infringed upon. The programming is so pervasive that it can sometimes take years to know how to think properly about freedom. This is why some will read the words on the previous pages and be upset about them. They will write this work off as insane because of those ideas that are radical. Those are merely a few thoughts as to the extent that freedom minded individuals should be willing to go in order to secure or simply live within that freedom. It is radical, but only because you are conditioned to think about how the state might respond; you may even fear them.

Recently I talked with someone who asserted that even though we want things to improve we are living in an age that enjoys more freedom than any age previously has known. They spoke about how advantage and opportunity is so great now that being alive and among western culture is like winning the lottery. This is not an uncommon statement among people these days and perhaps in many ages prior to it. While I agree with the idea that we do enjoy a type of freedom and we do have some advantages in this time period, I do not agree that we are nearly as better off as this propagandized view supposes. When I stated this to the man he became angry with me and even accused me of being an ungrateful jerk who simply doesn't appreciate any of the sacrifices people have made to give me the advantages I have.

The outburst at first surprised me but then it clicked, the programming of the state was so strong that speaking against what the state is supposedly providing, creates a sort of anger that can only be compared to religious fervor. Citizens will actually become angry and even violent toward people who do not believe that the state has provided and is providing freedom. Soldiers are taught to go to war and fight for freedom and if you speak out against them they will become violent with you defending the actions of the state! These actions are proposed to be what allows you to say the awful things you are saying.

First let me say that I do not fault anyone for becoming statist, they are brainwashed and it is tough to overcome that. I do not look down on soldiers or even police; I simply do not trust them. I know that in the right situation I could be acting in a completely non violent manner having violated no one and the state could send any one of their soldiers or officers to collect me in a way that would violate my rights and my safety as an individual. They would do this without regard to me and only under the banner of following orders. I do not fault them for thinking this way; but they are certainly guilty for being this way. In other words; I understand that they merely believe lies from the state but they are still guilty for their own involvement and for trusting the state so foolishly.

It is important that we recognize a distinction here. By feeling that they are scum for being cops or soldiers you cut off the possibility of converting them to liberty minded freedom fighters. If you can put your own emotion aside and simply learn to help them recognize what freedom looks like they might see their actions for what they are and turn from them. This is a huge victory for liberty and it is happening all the time. It cannot happen if we remain angry or judgmental toward people who simply thought they were doing something good. At the same time you cannot allow anyone to go on in the illusion that they are doing good when they are only an agent for the moral compass of another.

This is the problem with the state, it is like suggesting that their moral compass is better than the individual and so they have that control to determine which actions are acceptable. The state often proves that they are incapable of good actions and who is better to be a witness to this fact than those who do now or have worked directly with and for the state? Give them a place of refuge from that refuse.

Let's address our current freedom and why I don't buy into this idea that we are currently at the pinnacle of social freedom. I am at the time of writing this, in 2017 a 37 year old male in the U.S. I have seen many new laws go into effect in the past 20 years, the past 10 years, and even the past 5 years. These laws have not increased our liberty in that time they have limited them. There have been increasing gun restrictions, stiffer drug laws, more travel restrictions, intrusions on privacy, and so on and so forth for as long as I have been able to notice them. Now and again something lets up in one area but in five other areas a law tightens the noose around the neck of citizens restricting everything they do. There are more law enforcement now than there were ten years ago, more agencies in fact.

So I am supposed to believe and accept that we are freer than any society previously when in fact I have witnessed more laws and fewer freedoms throughout my life? Furthermore, I do not accept that the freedoms enjoyed a few years after the revolutionary war in this country were less than they are now. I know that perhaps some classes of citizens had more freedom than others but I also know that this is an argument against government not for it. Citizens had more freedom then than citizens do now and the only reason everyone couldn't be a citizen was because the government was restrictive... and they should not be... now or then.

If there is any hope that a people can live free than we are going to need to understand that freedom is not being experienced. I am not ungrateful for being born now, I have the opportunity to disseminate this message easier now than ever before but that is because of enterprise and capitalism, not government. I have more of an opportunity than ever before to witness a revolution of the mind that turns slaves into citizens of a world who know that they were born citizens; born with a right to themselves, and willing to protect that right for others born on this planet. It is imperative that we recognize that freedom does not exist within the state, it always exists within the mind and it is in the mind that we need to revolutionize what a society actually is and is not. It is merely a collection of people whose rights as groups are no greater or less simply because there are more of one and less of another.

If you think that you are free than go out and start a bank. Try to go out and start a bank and lend money to people who want to borrow, do this without having to ask permission and without having to pay for a license. Go and open any business you can think of without asking permission; if you get away with it I want you to connect with other Ancaps and teach them how but I know that it won't be long before you are dealing with some restrictions.

If you recognize that you are not free, then we can work with that. If you understand that physically you are not free but mentally you always have been, we can build from that. If you understand that underneath it all; humans crave freedom and the right to do what they would like to do as individuals and even groups; then we might be able to become free together.

SETTLEMENTS

It is extremely important that we acquire land. This is true of the individual and even truer of the group. Families would do well to leverage their collective resources for the sake of community development. You will probably be living near other people so you may as well choose to live near people with similar outlooks. It is also true of companies. Businesses and companies need to do as much as they can to own as much property as they can in particular areas. If pockets of people acquire lands together more can be done to subvert the claims that townships and governments place on those who are for liberty.

One idea worth looking into is to buy old towns that occasionally come up for sale. Even buying an old ghost town and turning it back into a village is an idea worth looking at. Additionally you can buy up most of the homes in new subdivisions or even build a small subdivision yourself with a collection of people. I have also come across old military bases for sale online. Here is a decent resource: http://www.missilebases.com

The advantage here is that security has already begun for you, it can be a great place for the right buyers, and you can possibly build multiple homes and even utilize the underground spaces for numerous apartments. Commercial real estate is a good place to find apartment complexes and even old commercial facilities that can be converted into communities that will benefit you and fellow Ancaps.

One of the personal goals of my family and I has been to grow a business that can build underground and below grade homes. We hope to be able to build master planned communities with this as our premise. As developments become more and more crowded going underground seems like a logical solution. There is more space utilized per parcel and if you desire you can use the space above the home as the

yard itself. One resource available now that can help is:
http://www.subsurfacebuildings.com

However you move forward it is necessary to realize that settlements are an important aspect. It is one thing to say that people should recognize the importance of self ownership and freedom and another thing altogether to begin to provide a community where people can live those principles. I don't propose that every aspect of a free society will be available but I am suggesting that we can never fully have a free society without a concerted effort of groups of individuals demonstrating that society.

Too often what comes to mind are military compounds where all sorts of questionable things are occurring. I have already revealed that I believe we need to do things that people consider questionable now; so long as we are not violating the liberty of others. Even with that belief I am suggesting that most of these settlements need to be completely above board and merely great places to spend your time and raise your families. They should be welcoming and inviting so that people can begin to recognize that Ancapistan is ultimately the very best place that people can live in a free society. If the majority of the settlements people see are drab and unwelcoming compounds of a military nature we will be grouped together with that sort of anarchist band of misfits that merely victimizes individuals. We are so anti victim that it is coming out of our ears and so people need to come to know that living in peace is achievable in a free society with Anarcho Capitalistic goals.

MILITATE & DEFEND

      This is a great time to roll into the subject of militias and defense of our networks and communities. Although the majority of our settlements should not be military like compounds we should have a somewhat active militia and private security companies. They certainly do not need to be fearsome things in the community but simply operated in the way any modern security company is. The key difference between our agents and other companies is the initiation of force. Most of the actions taken will be simply to seek restitution for harm and to remove people who are not welcome. Because we are within the boundaries of a social order that is now controlled by the state it may be necessary for our security companies to hand over certain violators such as murderers and the like to the proper authority. I say this with a grain of salt, although I have no love for the state and believe that all problems can and should be handled in house; I do not wish for the movement to be destroyed by aggressors who come after us only to destroy us. If someone crosses a known legal line that could potentially ruin the entire community if it appears it was covered up; we need to use extreme caution and in some cases throw them out to the wolves in the state.

Another form of defense is legal defense. If you can afford to train lawyers on the system that exists you should do just that. Although most of what we do will be to subvert the law we will require lawyers to defend people who are arrested by the state thugs and we will require lawyers who can share all of the legal loopholes and advantages that are available in each place we live and grow. There needs to be resources available to the laymen for building and protecting his family and his community in each place that they decide to settle.

It is tricky to go as far as saying that we need people in government offices, this may be true but extreme caution needs to be taken. Historically the individual who makes a valid attempt at entering public office to effect any positive changes becomes swallowed by a lifetime of political moves that are contradictory for the sake of some perceived positive effect. Most of the time they would have been better off living the Ancap life than to be playing pretend at it while "in service" to the public. Especially if they are taking a paycheck for that service, they are merely a member of the welfare state; being paid with stolen money.

Let's remember that we need to stockpile weapons on every occasion that we can. The Ancap community needs access to weapons whenever they want them. You never know when you will need to defend yourself from the statist thugs. There should be legal gun shops run by Ancaps and of course the under the table shops. I do not need to tell you that many people who are now Ancap might be restricted from gun ownership for some reason or another. This is a complete and total violation of the rights given to you, not only by your agency as an individual who owns themselves, but even by your own governments. The drafters of the constitution did not add restrictions for gun ownership they said that it should be protected at all cost. Not only for hunting and personal protection either. Gun ownership was all about responding to an aggressive government with the use of force. I am not advocating open attacks against the government I am merely saying that the drafters of the constitution were. In any event, having access to guns and ammo is a must.

Plan your security, both for your homes, your businesses, and every aspect of your life. If you do not plan your security you run the risk of being a victim. Perhaps you have no interest in guns; well you should still consider ways to defend yourself and your property. Be creative, cameras and general security measures are fine but don't be afraid to utilize more unconventional methods of protection. Electric fences are fun and you can obtain one at your local farm shop or order it online. They are non lethal and are an added level of security. I would suggest that you post warnings that the fence is hot to both warn a casual passerby and the potential

fence hopper. If you utilize anything
lethal in this sort of defense I would be
sure and proceed with caution, this sort
of thing is not legal anywhere that I know
of, plus it is possible that you can hurt
humans or animals in an unjust way; things
happen that might cause someone to
enter your property such as tripping,
crashing a bike or car, or even the
need to avoid another accident. I for
one would recommend sticking with
more conventional security measures; I
guess I am a purist on this subject.

COMMUNITY CREATION

Beyond the nuts and bolts of a community; whether it be one family, or many; you should consider the culture. Building a community whether at a single location or by connecting networks of people takes a lot of cultural factors that many may not consider. What is important to your particular brand of family or friends? You see, it is not just important that you agree to protect the freedom of others; you need to realize that a real life is being built.

I am not going to go on record saying that Ancap culture is this way or that way; it is whatever way people want it to be and the most diverse of communities. Virtually every culture can be represented so long as no culture is centered on enslaving another. Even in that case you would not limit the existence of such a culture; you would merely be weary of it and defend against it with every tool you have.

Culture is important because we are going to be raising children that need to have an understanding of

159

freedom. They are going to be somewhat exposed to a society that is totally against freedom and it is going to seem appealing in some ways. Nothing is necessarily limited from them; they should in fact have more available to them than the average citizen. They simply need to have exposure to people who can understand them and where they are coming from. If your child is home schooled you still might want them to have a social network, having a network of other parents who are Ancap will help them to grow socially. They can have sports teams and do activities and fit more seamlessly into a society that they are ultimately contrary too.

The children will have to choose to be free, you cannot just expect them to choose this, they will have to understand it in the same way everyone has. If a child becomes disenchanted by their community and its culture they will adopt the culture of the people around them. Unfortunately, the surrounding communities are very good at brainwashing citizens and appealing to the whims of the youth. The problem is that this culture does not have their best interest in mind, it wants to enslave them.

It is not a small thing to design a culture that your family can grow up under. Whatever your culture is now can help you to build a way to encourage it among your family and friends. At the same time you can simply take on some of the cultural aspects of the people that you know and respect. This may seem confusing but it really is pretty simple.

Hobbies are often a good indicator of culture. Some people may enjoy art, theatre, and music. Others may find that motorsports, water sports, or some other active venture is more satisfying. The types of people who spend time doing any of these things together tend to be building communities that grow together through these experiences. For them, living together or in the same neighborhoods may not even be a thought but they still spend a lot of time interacting with one another. If we come together for political purposes that ultimately offer the best example of a society and add to that strong culture; our cause will mature far beyond any political spectrum that has previously existed.

MONOPOLIES?

As long as there is no monopoly on force I suspect we shall have little to concern ourselves with. A monopoly can really only exist in an environment where people are not free to do what they choose. If anyone can start a company without restrictions then it is pretty hard to say that a monopoly will exist; if I don't like something I start a better company. Of course there may be some who are better at one business than others and the cream will rise to the challenge but they can only remain on top in a capitalistic environment if they remain good at what they do.

If you think that monopolies are not present now; think again. The state is the monopoly. The municipality holds a monopoly over resources such as water and sewer. You don't have another choice as to that cost, you pay the provider in your area or you don't get the utility. Electric companies are supposedly "privatized" because you can choose your supplier. This is such a huge joke in the industry; you pay the delivery to your local company regardless of who your supplier is. The person who puts the power line up and offers it should be the one you are paying. If multiple companies produce power and use lines put in place by another company they could easily pay a rental fee to that company and simply charge you based on their total costs.

The point I am making is that the government pretending to be breaking up the monopoly of the power company supply chains didn't really change anything; they simply created an environment where more people could cash in on this monopoly. Regulation itself is what stifles the progress of competition and today we have a power grid that is partially regulated and partially deregulated which is just a more palatable way of saying, "The whole thing is regulated and controlled... we just want you to feel like you had a choice."

Is it any different with any other portion of the state? They give you the illusion of choice when it comes to political ideology, the illusion of choice when it comes to education for your children, the illusion of choice when it comes to tax rates, and the illusion of choice in every other thing that is actually manipulated and controlled by the state. The state is the monopoly and it is the one monopoly that actually requires a real and true deregulation.

Throughout the 17 and 1800s slavery was somewhat common in the U.S. Black men and women were traded and treated as commodities by their owners. The right to themselves that they were endowed with was not given to them. I think we can all agree that many of these people were treated badly even inhumanely. What about the ones who were treated well? What about the people who were better off in the Americas than in the regions they had come from? Can you assume that some slave owners were better to their slaves than others, treating them almost as good as family members? I suppose this behavior is what eventually created an atmosphere where men who owned slaves began to detest the behavior as they recognized the life and the humanity in these people. Does it really matter how well a slave is treated? If a slave is treated well does it actually justify the act itself? I am saying that it certainly does not. I am saying that no matter how well you treat a person, claiming ownership over them makes them your slave, which is detestable and should be stopped.

Look at this nation. This is a nation filled with slaves. People who actually believe that because they can choose the type of car, the size of their television, and the clothes they wear; that they are free. This is a poor definition of freedom; it's irrelevant to say that you are freer than the slaves in the next town over, you are still not free if someone else has a monopoly over your production, and your very life. The state alone takes this liberty from you. No one else is allowed to have such a monopoly because you wouldn't put up with it for long; only the state has it because they have convinced you that you have a choice.

MUH ROADS!

Who is going to build the roads? This is satire of course. There are multiple questions that begin with, "Without government how will we_____?" The people saying these things may be just as genuine as can be but they are still naïve.

There are very little public works departments and those that exist are not all that efficient at their jobs. Let's take the post office for example; they routinely lose money and require continued public funds even though the price to mail a letter or package keeps going up. In contrast, companies such as FedEx and UPS continue to make a profit and grow while finding ways to lower costs on certain types of packages over others. Not only that they have contracts from the post office to deliver certain things and they sometimes pay the post office to deliver their items. If the whole thing was privatized you would have less people going POSTAL over how inefficiently the place is run.

In the case of roads specifically the people working on them are not government employees most of the time, they are employees of government sounding companies that have contracts with the state. In fact most "government" infrastructure is built in this way. Not only is this the case with infrastructure it is also true with the military. Companies such as Boeing, and Lockheed Martin have government contracts to build planes and military equipment. Many times the government will use multiple machine shops to make parts for classified devices, they pay the shop to make one item and the shop owner doesn't know what it is or what it is for he simply gets paid to follow the specs. They do this so that only a select few will know what something is or how to manufacture it.

So if the government themselves is not doing this, what are they doing? Well really they are simply taking your money and spending it the way they think they should. They are essentially saying that the public is not very good at spending their money on the things they need. Certainly there are people who don't spend wisely but most of the people who own homes, cars, and businesses seem to know how to spend their money. They spend on maintenance, supplies, resources, and anything else they need or want. Have you ever looked at what the government pays for things in comparison to the public? Some reports claim that a toilet seat in the white house costs taxpayers $30,000. I can't substantiate that claim but it wouldn't surprise me, no doubt it is tough to find the clear answer. Another report put the figure for the Obama family expenses in the year of 2012 at 1.4billion dollars... for just one year of expenses. The British royal family in the same year only cost their taxpayers 57.8 million. Doesn't that raise any eyebrows about the opulence of a position that is absolutely unnecessary? Yet people still believe that their money is being spent on all of this necessary infrastructure and defense from the boogie men in other countries. It is spent on presidential vacations and opulent living.

There are multiple ways to pay for the roads and plenty of people have answered these questions effectively. I will give but a few examples for you to chew on. Companies who sell anything that they want you to buy, will happily help pay for a road to get you to their door. Companies, who want to sell something, will pay for advertising along those highways you are driving. People, who want to go places, will help pay for roads because they do not want the cars they paid for to be destroyed by crappy roads. Companies, who sell you cars, will want you to drive places and so they will happily support an infrastructure for you to drive on. Some companies will come along who will make better quality private roads that have more amenities than others; which charge a toll or a subscription for you to utilize them.

This is but a small pebble in the vast range of ideas that can be obtained when you take away the restriction of the state and begin to think for yourself about how to solve problems. The state has not been solving problems very good even with our tax money. Roads and infrastructure suffer while the president rolls around in a fancy jet with many guards protecting him because he is an asshole that most people, or at least a large group of people, don't like. It doesn't matter who the president is... people won't like him because on some level we know that positions of power like that are ridiculous.

As for military defense spending, most of the foolishness about boogie men in other countries coming to get us is manufactured to control people with fear. Other times we have been over there with our freedom fighters killing women and children and so we create enemies where there would otherwise have been none.

In the same way we can solve this privately with logic. Most citizens want to be protected and will choose to pay for some form of defense. Most citizens will even help to defend themselves and other citizens when push comes to shove. I always see these arguments where some evil villain is going to try to subjugate the masses but people fail to recognize that the government is that villain who has made themselves palatable to the society they subjugate. When you deal with people on a one on one basis in public, there are very few super villains who are trying to be super violent toward you. There are some... but they are disposed with now and will be disposed with more freely in a free society.

Virtually every problem that you can lift out of your mind for why freedom without government cannot work is answerable by that same mind applying itself to market based solutions. If you can find the answer you're Ancaping! If you can at least brainstorm some market based solutions you are Ancap like most humans at their core, and you will go places in that society that you are restricted from going in this one.

FREE ENTERPRISE AT LAST

Can we take a sigh of relief? Can we let out that long held breath of hope and know that finally we are going to depend on human innovation to solve the problems of humanity? Innovation does not exist within a restricted environment, it is limited twice; once by the mind that can come up with something and secondly by the mind that needs to ask permission to do it.

Give yourself permission and then ask forgiveness. Fuck that... sorry for the F bomb but I mean it... don't ask for forgiveness just tell them it was none of their business to begin with and go and do what you want. If you victimize someone you will soon become someone's victim, if you don't you will just be a human doing what human's do... being free.

Much of the world is ready for freedom. Some people may not be ready for it and those people can just stay in bondage if that's what they want... but some of us are ready... we simply need to begin to live it. We need to

173

build networks of people who believe in self ownership, individual freedom, and market freedom. If you are one of these people and you can identify with even a portion of what is being presented then take action and Join us:

https://www.facebook.com/groups/1239950219415983/

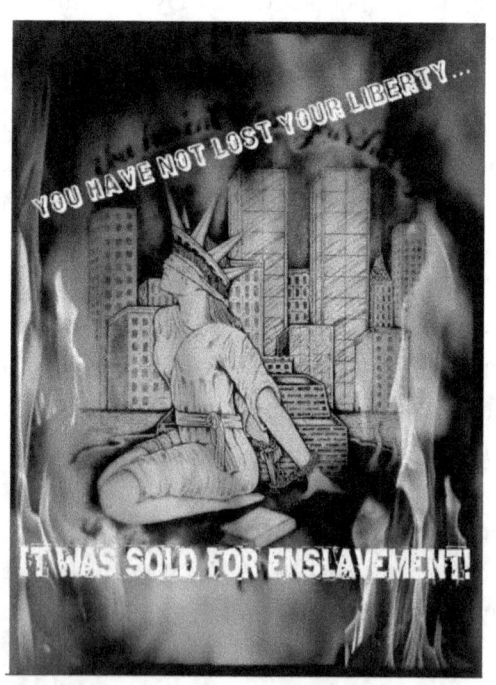